Burning It Down

Burning It Down

Dancing in the Rubble

Neelam Patel

New Degree Press

Burning It Down
Dancing in the Rubble

ISBN 978-1-63730-814-1 *Paperback*
978-1-63730-876-9 *Kindle Ebook*
978-1-63730-974-2 *Ebook*

I dedicate this book to myself.

Specifically, to the future version of me who will emerge

after making and sharing this work.

Contents

"You only are free when you realize you belong no place—you belong every place—no place at all. The price is high. The reward is great...More and more, I belong to myself. I'm very proud of that."

MAYA ANGELOU

Author's Note: The Relief of Imperfection

In 2020, I burned it all down to write this poetry book. I left my twenty-two-plus year career in high tech to dive into my creative life with full force. When I intentionally slowed down my pace and didn't have the distraction of a whole job, I was left with a singular challenge: face myself.

This challenge was tricky because it was crowded in my head; I'd absorbed so many perspectives from other people, that my throat became a carrier for bootlegged ideas. In fact, I *actively avoided* any uncomfortable thoughts and feelings by feeding my addiction to "cool experiences." Every city I traveled to around the world meant a chance to collect amazing stories: I dared myself to befriend strangers, perform improv dances in public, and had a knack for turning ordinary moments into memorable adventures. This tendency went so far that one actor friend joked that she didn't need to see any shows, because she could sit down to dinner with me and wait for my signature: "*Wanna hear a story?*"

But I'm not a story. And the whole setup was a tragedy because when I skip over my ill-branded "negative feelings," I lose access to all good sensations too. It is all made worse by the "healing tension" that permeates social media. Specifically, I was exhausted from being talked out of my uncomfortable feelings like shame or rage by powerful inspirational talks that only reveal the before and the so-called "after." Talks like this go something like: "I felt embarrassed about being from a different culture and wanted to hide it. And now that I'm a full-grown adult, I feel empowered and grateful for my differences." Hearing these stories made me feel admiration, but also a definite sense of being "not enough," because what about the young girl inside of me who is still hurt? Do I shove her back inside and pretend I feel fine? It's this "shoving back" that adds tension to the healing. It's the monster of all monsters—my shame about the shame. And, the entire time, I am not acknowledging the vast and wide-open space where I truly am, and where we all are hanging out—the middle.

The messy middle.

This book is about staying curious a little longer about the messy middle, and hopefully un-shaming the shame. If I am on a kayak trip, the awesome paradox is that it is only when I embrace my wet underwear and my sloshy socks, allowing the utter discomfort into my being, that I can relax, and enjoy the view. In other words, it is letting the shame sting a little that is the passageway to all the good feelings like gratitude, love, joy. I learned that the light is not at the end of the tunnel – it is in the goopy, messy, complicated middle.

If we are all here in the middle anyway, then my intention is to celebrate it and even dance in life's gorgeous rubble.

Do. Not. Worry. This book is not about staying in the discomfort forever (ouch). It is about the transformation that comes from allowing our unpleasant feelings to simply exist, instead of shaming them back into stress with mean and unhelpful self-judgements like *"You should be over it by now."* In fact, I am a transformation junkie at heart. My therapist once told me that my poems *were* my therapist because they carry me into seeing a new view. So, it is my hope that they bring a moment of expansion to others as well. Creating this space to exist as-is, in whatever state we find ourselves in, makes us more expansive as individuals. This, in turn, lets us connect with one another in real ways, instead of doubling down on our loneliness and missing each other in plain sight. If our souls are homes, then it is my ambition that my work strengthens our floorboards, unhinges forgotten windows, and adds inches to our ceilings.

How does someone like me accept this challenge of facing myself, and to create this expansive space, after making it a point to avoid it at all costs? It turns out I have a helpful superpower—I can feel everything. All. The. Time. Some call it having thin skin, but I say there's a lot more to it. I could literally point to a body part and listen for the vibrations I receive from it and type out a vivid poem. Many of the poems in this book were created exactly this way. This book is my way of honoring this superpower and honoring myself. In each poem, I shine a flashlight on a particular facet that I wish to sit with and witness, oftentimes uncomfortable. It is my privilege to have your presence upon these facets too. I have included poems that are autobiographical, as well as others that are flights of my imagination inspired by conversations and research.

Why do I want to do all of this?

I want to live like I write in my poem, ***"I want to be just a little bit dangerous,"*** "I want to paint my fingernails in my real desire," and "walk like I just picked an apple off a tree I grew myself and ate it whole—skin, seed, core and all." By accepting my feelings as-is, I can live my life in full color, in 360 degrees.

I also felt it was extremely important to ***acknowledge how difficult and plain frightening this work is***, as can be found in the poem "The Danger of Vulnerability," where I demand "What if I need you? What if I hitchhike into my life, with a soft thumb exposed, and you run me over with your fucking truck, wipe me out, before even asking where I was heading?"

Most of all, ***I want to un-shame the shame.*** In fact, I attempt to do that in specific ways with my "Beautiful Shame" series, which are three poems that describe shame as internal electric fences, keeping us enclosed inside of ourselves; and how I had to experience the sting of their charge, to free myself. Ultimately, I rebrand my electric fences as my very gateways to a more unbound life.

Finally, I desire to expose ***how Peace entered the chat for me***. The more I dug into myself, the more I encountered opposing qualities coexisting—murderous rage and deep love, masculine and feminine, calm and menace. My internal forces can be, and likely always are, quite intensely opposing, but I do not have to live "in opposition." In fact, I can aspire to live in peace by welcoming all my opposing feelings to the same Thanksgiving table of my vast being, and even feeding them well, letting each distinct quality live its fullest expression. The goal is to live like my turtle does in "Turtle Poem"; she retreats into herself for acceptance and comfort, rather than hiding from fear or shame.

My poems celebrate the messy middle wherever you are in life, with focus on areas like following your dreams, speaking up for yourself, the varying textures of an immigrant experience, rage as an everyday ally, thriving and enjoying sexuality after assault (*the poems about sexual assault are marked with a sun held by a hand. I trust survivors will know what they need to feel contained*), the subtleties of making and grieving friendships, a woman's body as a place of prowess, an insider's view of brown skin color as it relates to self-acceptance, and alternative ways of integrating meaningful self-care.

This book is my way of inviting you to pull up a chair as I let my old paradigms burn in flames, so I can make space for more layered truths underneath. Bring some marshmallows. I've got the fire covered. There's plenty of space out here in the imperfect middle—tons and tons of it. What a relief.

Dance with me in the rubble?

Trigger Warning:

In the spirit of psychological safety. I've marked those pieces which may activate experiences of sexual trauma with the symbol shown here. I trust survivors will follow their own needs to feel contained and nourished.

Navigating the Book

Heroine's Journey

During the writing process, I happened to attend a South Asian women's group where I learned about the story construct called the Heroine's Journey by Maureen Murdock, and I quickly realized that my poetry fell into this structure quite naturally. I believe the reason that happened is because making this book was about 50 percent collecting poems I'd already written since 2003 almost twenty years ago, and about 50 percent composing new material. The combination of the two sets of material led to this natural arch of experiencing spiritual wholeness.

The first four chapters of the Heroine's Journey reflect the traditional linear Hero's journey that Joseph Campbell popularized and upon which many movies, such as *Star Wars*, are based on. Specifically, the chapters are 1) Separating from the feminine instincts to make it in the world, 2) Gathering allies and getting mentally prepared for life's hustle in a man's world by aligning with the masculine side. 3) Fighting dragons & facing obstacles on the road, and 4) Enjoying the favor of success.

We go deeper in Chapters 5–10, which is the Heroine's Journey of witnessing the uncomfortable and disparate parts of oneself and merging them into a more expansive being. Specifically, those chapters appear as 5) Awakening to spiritual aridity, 6) Descent into the goddess and facing shadows, 7) Urgent yearning to reconnect with the abandoned feminine side, 8) Healing the mother/daughter split, 9) Healing the wounded masculine, and 10) Integration of the masculine (focused on being something) with the feminine (desiring to just be).

This journey represents the cyclical nature of living. While there is a succession mapped out in sequential chapters, the reality is that these emotional states can be enlivened at various times, and we can even be living in multiple states for various inner journeys (like career, a specific relationship, or body acceptance) at the same time. ***There is no right way or correct order to experience this book.***

Make no mistake, the Heroine's Journey is something all humans—men, women, or those beyond the binary—can, and probably should, experience. If we are constantly shoving our inner man or inner woman inside from shame, then we are living in tension. We all contain both, thank goodness.

Engaging with the Book

Ultimately, how you engage with the book is, and should be, entirely your choice. I hold a light to different rooms inside my being. Sometimes I simply notice the room exists, and that makes sufficient space to live in the present moment more fully. Similarly, I invite you to decide how you wish to engage. Some days, you may want to experience my rage poems, for example, by simply noticing your own rage door and feeling a hint of expansion and relief by having taken that small bit of space as you go along in your day. Other times, you may wish to open the door, walk in, and pull up a chair to immerse yourself in it with me, honoring your full capacity.

The point of the book is to acknowledge some of the multitudes of inner rooms, each with their own distinct vibrations that are at play. The amount of space we make for them depends on a lot of things, and only you are the expert on what you have capacity for and what you desire. As Rumi so gorgeously says: "*We rarely hear the inner music, but we're dancing to it nonetheless.*"

If you dive into the shadows with me, I challenge you to bring along a pen, a journal, and a good playlist. In fact, if you prefer a journal guide to get an idea of how I made my way through the work, there is a free list of journal prompts available at **www.tailoredpoetry.com/my-book**. If you're a poet, you can use them as poetry prompts. If you wish to share your work, feel free to tag me on my social media @ dancewithneelam. I highly recommend dancing or any sort of movement, even if it's simply shaking your arms or legs. Our bodies are amazing vehicles that can take us to where we are going, so long as we allow the vibration to move through us. I've shared my favorite playlists on that page too. Put on some music and let's shake it out!

Regardless of which route you take I also recommend some good hot chocolate as accompaniment. Why do I say that? I did most of my editing with hot chocolate in hand, so it would be a fun continuation of this book's life.

Finally, I have sprinkled in shorter, more aspirational poems, like "Choose Possibility" from Chapter 2, which is about living with a sense of wonder, or "Luxury Accommodations" in Chapter 10, which is about living in the ever-changing present moment. I need both the shadow-facing poems as well as my more aspirational visions to feel collected while I settle into my rubble. One without the other isn't sustainable; diving only into shadows makes life too heavy, and exploring only the aspirations feels untrue and, worse, full of tension from hiding my true more layered self. One of my favorite aspirational poems is "Giraffe Poem", which proclaims that a giraffe is beautiful not because she is tall, but rather because she "commits to staying lifted" and because she breathes from "her highest, her most inspired, her only self."

Heroine's Journey Chapter 1:

Separating from the Feminine

In this chapter, the Heroine is feuding with her own feminine side to make it in a man's world. If the symbolic archetype for her feminine side is the mother, then this stage is the initial shedding of her feminine layer, in rage against her mother for having taken on so much of the traditional feminine role.

The poems in this chapter have a theme of either separating from my female instincts or are reflective pieces around the realization that I must start aligning myself to my masculine side. They represent a point of clear separation and, in some cases, decision points in poetry form.

How it Happened: My Destiny's Naming Ceremony

Stars tell the secret
of which sounds
a baby's name
should start with.

The town's mystic looks up to the blue
and down to a vibrant Indian earth
at my birth, reads my horoscope,
pronounces which sounds should start my name,
which vibrations can identify me,
to promise me my best destiny.
B, V, U—this cluster of sounds, always assembled together,
are cast into the clear air.

My mother selects V for me,
names me Vibha—which means night.
Night—when India sends the moon
to America,
and America passes back the sun
to India.

In the US, it's not the stars, but the ticking clocks
that chart our lives.
Time is a target to be hit, carved out, punched in.
Immigration, Customs & Borders, schedules no
naming mystics.
I am packaged up in a manila folder—
official papers all stapled together.
A blank line denotes who I am.

My father, already in the states, speeds through the
form-filling,
faces an empty space for my name.
He looks up to summon something.

Stars can't talk.
India's secret sound for me is stowed away in silence,
suspended in the air between two countries.
My mother keeps my name in her chest and on her lips—
no telephones
in the village where I am born.

My father has to write down a name,
make it up, force it out from the ground up
before Time is up. tock tock tick tick.
He picks Neelam.
Spells it out with his pen to get it done,
before he even says it to anyone.
5 months old—I arrive in an airport in Chicago
with my mother, all wrapped up
in a stack of documents with my name on it.

Stars that once sang out "Vibha,"
invoking a night's moon,
suddenly lose their luminosity
to city lights, concrete streets,
and deadlines.

A Little Bit Dangerous

I was afraid
of sticking out.
Built a rubber wall
so I would bounce back inside
and not hurt anyone.
No one gets scraped inside of a rubber wall.

My brain is a fear-making machine;
SPITS OUT THOUGHTS
IN ALL CAPS, IN BLEEEEEEEDING INK
LIKE A PRINTER   GO
NE MAD
Good thing paper-thin thoughts can be trashed.

I'll paint my fingernails red, real, ravishing.
Pluck an apple off a tree I planted myself,
eat it whole—red skin, seeds, core, and all.
Watch as I expand instead of explain.
I know I have access to my own joy,
because I become the music when I dance.

I'll bound outside these rubber walls.
Taking, making, consuming space.

I want to be just a little bit
dangerous.

Aggressive like the Spring

Be aggressive like the spring.

With unmatched ecstasy,
spring penetrates straight into wintertime
using the strength of her own volition,
force.

Cherry blossoms celebrate, sprouting into a full rally.
a welcoming committee of yellow trumpet daffodils
bursts out into the open,
the purple iris rises into her light, her dignity.

Each flower forces color into plain sight, unworried
whether earth's canvas can handle her palette,
her pleasure.
Pushing, pushing
out from all the places that enclose her,

so she may witness her own blooms,
smell her own scent,
sing her own songs,
swing in the open air,
be seen.

Glory to the Springtime,
Glory to the Ambitious Woman,
Glory to the Aggression that causes colorful gardens,
lush landscapes,
whole countries.

Good Pride

The peacock
claims his divinity.

Flames out his fan of colors,
waves back to the gods.

On radiant display,
unhesitant.

I am Strong

I didn't notice the complete battalion
at the ready, inside my belly,

persistently announcing my battle cries,
advancing with artillery in hand.

I am not made to shatter like glass.

All along, **I was praying for the strength I already had.**

Coral Reef

Don't look to me as pink jewelry.
I am also breathing for my life,
just like you.

My shape and beauty
are my protection
and power.

You can enjoy me,
but you may not
consume me.

True Trunk

You stood as my tree trunk,
so I could let my branches
bend so far, and let my leaves
fly.

I want to forget you.

I am making my own core solid,
strong. You were never my true
trunk, you just let me foresee
my own firmness to come.

And as for me, I was not your greenery
nor your rainwater either.
I was not the channel in your
underwater map, leading you
to your tears, and all your vulnerability.

I was just your mirror
in my dangling earrings,
where you could see your own leaves
take flight.

Dealer, Deal Me Out

I wake up and find myself at a poker table.
Everyone is playing their "pretty" cards.
Jack of eyeliner.
King of high heels.
Queen of diamond earrings.
Ace of comparison.
All eyes on me.
I look around the table,
and smile with triumph glossed on my lips,

I fold.

I put my cards face down on this table where nobody wins,
because nobody exhales.
I'm now gambling for my natural flow,
the way I know I need to glow.
I play to win
my own hand.

I see a table of mascara eyes.
Their long nails are polished perfectly,
but the scraping of self-judgement
is all mine.

I'll make my own deck—Jack of self-kindness,
Queen of my intuition, King of my personal authority.
All hearts in my stack.

Dealer, deal me out.

Q
Q

K
K

Hero in the Mirror

I am not a damsel in distress.
I put on my courage
before I put on my dress.

I am not my well-stitched skirt,
nor my great-fitting jeans.
My clothes are not the actual intrigue.

I apply my audacity,
before I select a lipstick.

Eagle Advice

The golden eagle
does not care
who stares
at her wingspan.
Why should you?

She advises:
Fly well,
and when you perch,
take up your entire seat,
high up in the trees where you are seen
clearly.

If your feathers shake as you greet your fans,
wondering, *Why me?*

Stay in your moment,
let your unsteady vibration mix
with your sturdy song of gratitude:

Thank you for trusting me.
Thank you for trusting me.
Thank you for trusting me.

Sing it to us,
sing it to yourself,
sing it to the entire forest.

see you in the water

i rotated my calendar month until it was upside down,
as if holding a familiar flower, growing from its root down
to its height.
each square day a window now
to look out and stare at wisps of clouds,
whispers of familiar crowded-out dreams

what if i decided to do it?

maybe the rising ocean wave stuck in neutral will find its
way to a cheering crash,
maybe piercing red lights turn bright green,
maybe yesterday and tomorrow are dried up leaves i can
exchange for today's fresh juice.

maybe i live in expansion,
relaxed but moving.
maybe i drop into a fully breathing life,

maybe i dance.

i take the path only my two feet can map. i take the lead
and i follow, follow, follow my heart.
i slip into my soul with sudden abandon, the kind that
leaves mango stains all over my face.

i put on a hard hat and work with confidence, the kind that
causes cities to rise upon rubble,
i surrender to my world with immense curiosity,

curiosity that causes laughter
to return to such cavernous wounds.

i move with freedom like rain that seeps through
overprotective umbrellas, onto my skin cells,
unlocking secret desires to be soaked, raw, ready,
making the forbidden feel natural.

i learn to settle into uncomfortable seats and advance into
awkward talks.
i undock my boat to send myself into unseen chapters
and towards the unknown faces of my newest
crewmates.

i will move, i will be moved.
i am taking the plunge.
see you in the water.

Heroine's Journey Chapter 2:

Identifying with the Masculine

In this stage, the Heroine knows the world is set up as a man's domain and aligns closely with her father. She seeks his approval, and the approval of other men, for her ability to make it in this world.

The poems in this chapter represent a deepening of my intention to fall in line with the masculine way of working. I create this place of strength by bolstering myself in moments of doubt. And I set up my world for achievement and success with my father as an important source of support—my original ally as I march into the workplace.

Eye Level

I step into the scene already in front of me,
and the word *yes* comes beaming out.
I edit out the parts where my eyes glance up, down, away,
and elsewhere.
I don't pretend to have lost it all,
when this replenishing gift lives
right in front of me—
this perfectly imperfect present moment,
that can only be collected at eye level.

I don't look up to mountain tops, or down to deep seas,
places where oxygen is hard to come by.
The movie of my life
is happening
already.
Right in front of me.

I only have to adjust my eyes
and inhale.
I was already cast—
This show is not a draft.
It is not carried in whisper.
My mic is already hot,
I am already on,
live,
in surround sound.
I don't wait for the credits to run to see proof of my being,
I don't wait for emergencies to reset my view.
This life already offered me a spot.

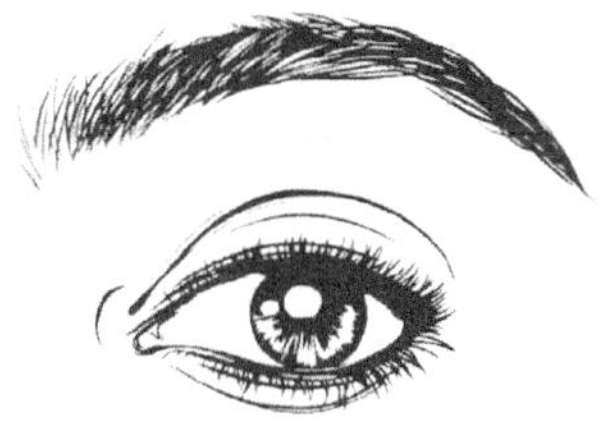

I'm already here.

I say yes to this lifetime.
I say yes
at eye level,
at I level.

How to Make a Wish

When you are yearning for a wish to come true,
light up your birthday candles again,
collect four-leaf clovers and take hold of lucky coins.
If the clock says 11:11, take a staircase straight to the stars;
possess them with your wish.

When the smoke from the candles reaches the angels,
and the four-leaf wish makes it to the other side of
the rainbow,
and the lucky coin is tucked into your pocket,
know that the sky is making a wish back,
wishing that you do what you never tried before,
something new,
to make the wish come true.

Ignite your wish with a fresh action
Wishes are not made of smoke.
They are deals you draw on earth.

Offer something up.
A firefly doesn't just wish to light up,
he does his part to fly so the night air can rush to his belly,
and ignite him.
He ensures his incandescence is inevitable,
conspiring together with the gods.

11 11

Choose Possibility

A snowflake,
on its way down,

is not aware that it could
one day become
the red juice of an unopened fruit, held perfectly inside of
a pomegranate.

Or that it might be carried bumpily in the curve of a camel
on a hot desert,
swishing horizontally.

Or that this snowflake might later find a surprise sway
dance deep inside an unknown part of the sea.

If you need something fresh, trust whatever ride
comes next.

Stick out your tongue,
let the next new chance land in your mouth,
melt, become a part of you.

Live impossibly
inside of possibility.

The Seduction of Winning

Winning is not an art form,
it is a plain decision to create a future, a destiny.
I won't wait for luck to come to me,
I will march straight into the light, to be crowned
winner.

Come with me to the island of winning.
The beds are lined with tropical flowers,
one purple, one pink, then indigo, then a new shade of red.
I will pick the scent of jasmine flowers,
and **smear their petals to your skin.**
to mark you winner.

There, we will sleep to an ocean's cradling.
and wake to the sounds of winning again.
Again, again, and again.

Just Like Constellations

A sky full of wonder pours down,
washes me in the miracle of being.

When I want to speak,
I do not seek tiny twigs from the ground,
grind them up, spit them out again, and again,
and yet again.

Before I talk,
I reach up for the heavenly galaxies and pause.
Wait to hear words that resound
with my northernmost star.

I amplify my wild connection to space,
even my banter is full of light,
and **my life's audio track,**
strung together, would feel
just like constellations.

But I say the wrong things all the time.
Words come out disfigured,
landing more like collision-course meteoroids
than beautiful falling stars.
I make mistakes, tying knots
instead of freeing up space to dream.

Then, I interrupt myself mid-sentence
to breathe, to stretch my mind up to the sky,
until I fall back into a starry arrangement.

Beautiful Composition

You wrote this composition in my body.
This melody, this music so raw,
I memorized every line, every measure, every note.
Every high-pitched saxophone crescendo squeals
out my excitement to see you.
The slow low bass holds my heart still.
I memorize the effects of the fast-paced piano solo, and the pause
            between
                        each
                                    drum
                                                strike.
I memorize the timing of the inhale breath of
each musician,
a breath full of animal instincts,
my own vessels and beginnings,
our laughter, and you.
I keep your stunning composition playing and playing
and playing inside of me.

A loud thought shocks me through my headphones,
shakes me awake from my musical daze:

The sound you vibrate inside of me
was my own sensuality
already in my veins

You may have woken it up,
but I get to keep it

after us.
It was never you
who made me sexy,
alive.

I use my free lungs
as a built-in metronome,
my nuanced feelings are sheets of soulful music,
my thoughts are an astute conductor.
Every organ is an instrument
that **pulses out a rhapsody,**
that is all me,

my own beautiful composition.

Measure the Sky

I used to deconstruct my life
take it apart like a clock,
carefully remove the batteries,
line up all the cogs and wheels
neatly on the floor,
examine and polish them,
so I can measure my stretch of time,
measure myself.

Now
I want to destroy
the machinery I made,
until I see nothing
but the dust of time,
a wide-open clearing
from where I can take up
all my space.

I was never "too much."

The materials with which we were measuring
were always too small.

I stop calculating my life
by the tiny stopwatch on your wrist.
I do not appraise my own pulsation.
I cannot measure my sky
with these small supplies I have
here on earth.

Love Poem to Money

Dear money,
I apologize for the moments I pretend
that you don't exist.
I was being so absurd, like saying
there's no water in the rain,
when you were pouring all over my mind, the whole time.

I apologize for the times I do
remember you, and
pour hateful vitriol,
cursing out your innocent ears
with ice cold whispers.

I kick the door with lead-tipped shoes,
the weight of my own shame
stubbing my toe.

My anger against you
is always my fear of losing you.

So, my hands are loose on you,
forecasting a drought as soon as I
see you in my account.

I live in the farce of scarcity,
believing only my lack could save me,
as if being bereft of money leaves me
with the shiny currency of Love.

You make me feel dumb.
Loitering in the hallway when I should be in class.
I feel shady pretending I am one hundred,
when I feel like zero, knowing so little about you.

My desire doubles my shame.
Does to make me dirty to want to be rich with you?
Does licking my fingers from my own harvest
turn someone else's sprinklers off?
Can it cast their land dry?
and won't that make me
filthy?

I've laid out a second welcome mat,
now my hate, shame, fear
have a place to land too.

Dear money,
Let's start again.
I'll do my part,
lavishing you with my highest love,
attention, and joy,
so you can come splashing in,
glistening in the sunlight.
Both my eyes are wide open,
you are a guest, I am the host.
I take the time to see you,
to receive you.

What if I Make You Jealous and I Like it?

I've already got my matchbook in my hands.

I used to feel so guilty
that you might feel bad,
if I am a badass,
that you could be jealous
if I succeed.

But, what if I savor it a little,
when I make you jealous?
Swirl that flavor for a little longer
as I let it linger on my tongue?

Would that make me the cause
of your darkness?
I stopped myself in my tracks
from the shame of that.

If someone said I was their archrival,
I would lay down, give them room
to run past, over, through me.

Humility would stop me
before I had anything to be humble about.

Now I want to light up the sky
with my fireworks.
If you're made to feel

Jealous
of my badassery;
and if that turns me on a little,
making me check my nails and smirk,
maybe that doesn't make me
a slight bitch or a total jerk.

I was never stepping into your light,
I was never stepping on top of your chest.
Your lane was always clear,

I no longer lay myself
down to rest in depression
in the middle of my own road.

My lane was always clear,
nobody can drive in it.

Look out, I'm lighting it all up.
I make my own commotion
for only one person — me.

I've already got my matchbook in my hands.

My Turn – when Assertiveness feels like Omnipotence

Get out from under my skin.

I'm not afraid to break your angles.
Your sharp penetrated thoughts.
Your precision.
Your ankles even.
With my kick.
Fuck you.

I'm done ducking and covering for myself.
I cannot go the distance
if I am not the one who is driving.

I've come here to make a move,
to run my life.
Get out.
Of my
motherfucking

way.

Indestructible

I was all marshmallow,
wanting only to be desired
and smooshed by kisses,
disappearing
by the burning
of your craving.

I was pretending
to be weak, hiding,
speaking like a mouse,
as if never meaning to be heard.

I was soft and edible,
sweetening everything.

But I am not a mish mash
of too much sugar.
I was not cast
into the celestial light
just to be
swallowed whole.

Take back your opinions.
I poured them on like melted chocolate,
too quick to my tongue.

Take back your views too,
the color of that one internet dress I see
is gold and white.

You sense the same one as blue and black,
we are both right, and we are not the same
entity.
Your world and mine
cannot be the exact same.

I stop diving into your mirror,
bending the light and
becoming a mirage of you.

I am not the marshmallow,
I am the fresh spark of every fire.

If I begin to melt, lose some of my sturdiness,
I recall that I can rekindle my authority,
I was always the flame.

I am more than royalty,
I can ignite my divinity,
take sovereignty
over my soul's entire territory.
Indestructible.

In the Hot Spring, a Poem about Perfectionism

Did you splurge all your time today,
or did you release into your moment?

Did you hold time hostage,
or did you get to open your gates?

Were you stingy with it,
holding it tightly even while you were giving it away?
Or did you let time fall through you,
like trees let sunlight through their leaves?

I won't negotiate with perfection, the scrooge of time,
or put its monstrosity on the shelf to haunt me later.
I'd rather pay my attention to the rich present moment,
the one that doesn't even understand your rulers
or your graphs.

Let the critics walk with their harsh clipboards,
ammunition to push you back into yesteryears.

Let us soak in the hot spring,
melt into the steam of the present moment.

Forgo the frigid air
where perfection speaks loudly,
using its signature nonsensical
nightmarish
jumbled up sentences.

The water is warm here.
We breathe in gulps of nutritious air,
and even laugh as we work.

Heroine's Journey Chapter 3:

Facing Dragons, a Road of Trials

In this stage, our Heroine continues her pursuits, but faces the inevitable challenges that arise as she is still a woman, making it in a man's world. She begins to face outer conflict that challenges her inner resolve. She finds herself with two minds—the one who can "push through" and "do anything" and the other who questions herself and her place.

The poems I include in this chapter represent my initial breaking points earlier in my career—challenges from outside reactions relating to my abilities, my appearances, my competition, and my self-confidence.

This Time, I am a Dragon

Send me back to old conversations
that faded my being
into an outline of me—
conversations with men
in the workplace.

This time, I am a dragon.

As I wait for a conference room door to open,
a man whispers seriously:
"You're new here, let me tell you something.
You're too prepared. You're making everyone look bad."

Instead of diminishing myself, limiting my output to 80%,
this time, my dragon mouth scorches him.
I defend my hoard of gold, this wealth
of intelligence, and shout:
"MOVE. I am not placed here to comfort you. I have
already soared off
from new cliffs before you even smelled your
morning coffee."

I reclaim my fortress,
fire finally comes out from my nostrils,
instead of letting it gut my own stomach.

At a cubicle, solving an engineer's project problem:
a man says:
"Oh, I didn't know you were smart. I mean, you're attractive."

Instead of questioning my too-much-ness and softening my voice,
this time my dragon body laughs at this tiny knight's tiny sword.
I defend my brightness, my intellect, my entire hoard.
"MOVE. I'm too busy lining my lips in black, so you can watch my words clearly.
If you can't handle me,
GO. THE. FUCK. AWAY."

I wave my dragon tail
like a sharp middle finger
at his memory.
I take back my territory.

During a lunch break with my work pal (a man),
he says, "You were right. People totally ignore your ideas in meetings, then someone else
says the same thing and everyone agrees." I respond: "Wow, thanks...how did you figure it out?"
he says: "Because I've been doing it ever since you told me."
Instead of letting it go, trying not to be the Difficult-Woman-at-Work,
this time, my dragon face incinerates his tongue into a ball of fire so massive,
I may have made a second sun
to shine on all women.

My dragon body
leads the way now.

There are no prisoners in my lair.
I aim all my jets of flames
directly into rusty old castles,
until they are piles of dust,
and crooked skeletons
with trembling skulls.

Men were never gods, now I see.
They are just people.

I am from Pangea

I am from Pangea.

That place before places, before words,
before humans.

My new answer is laced in bitterness,
and who can blame me?
I see clearly from the whites of my eyes:
When you ask me where I'm from,
originally,
your hungry finger scrapes my arm,
asking why it is so brown.

I am grounded to a halt in this familiar
conversational layover,
delayed and hoping to escape to a more relaxed path.
I am unable to un-claim my beautiful baggage.
I carry it all with me,
marching aimlessly,
inside my mind's terminal.

Fellow Americans interrupt our first conversation
with the word "*No*"
eating my response from out of my mouth,
when I attempt to answer where it is I am from.

I dig into powerless pits,
explaining and explaining
how my first memory was certainly from New Jersey.

Freedom does arrive,
but not from the land where bells of liberty can be cracked.
It is in Copenhagen where a bartender asks
"Where are you from?"
I say "Washington, DC."
Immediately my muscles all clench, preparing
for the toothy bite of the approaching interrogation, but
it never comes.
My shield melts into the silky luxury
of belonging.

Hammock, Song of my Skin Color

Come with me where the water is ice cold
and the beer is lukewarm.
Come with me where every shoe has a sharp stone inside.

Come with me to the lighthouse,
where the light is so bright but nobody sees you.
You dusted off your fog, your gloom, your dingy outlook—
well done.
But your face is too dark;
they only see shadows.

Come with me where the water is warm,
and the drinks are cool.
Come with me where the shoes are comfortable,
and the lounge seats are ready.

Come with me to the quiet lake,
where you can take hold of the doubt
that was sparked from outside of you,
where you can witness the question marks
others may have left on your skin.

Watch these thoughts fall through your hammock,
while **you stay suspended**
in your clarity, your sanity, your dignity.

Midnight Shadow

Tonight I put on a new shade of eye
shadow
too dark, smearing midnight onto my eyelids.
In the mirror, I see that I live in the dust of her trail,
imprisoned by a gorgeous sister.

Even her shadow is more confident than I.
My headquarters reside inside her.
I anticipate her moves, her thoughts,
her decisions.

It's impossible to get the timing right.
She moves left, I am pulled.
She moves right, I am tugged again,
but a second too late.

I can only house one soul,
not two.
How can I pour her being
into my body every day?
I became obscure coffee,
made from yesterday's used grounds,
holding only a hint of my own depth.

Lost because I gave her my compass.
I spend time with every mirror
to rearrange my dark skin cells into her
bright white glow.

Today I catch a glance in the glass
of someone else,
who is at ease, she dares me:

"Self, shadow me."

I see my left arm was never
attached to her body.

"Self, shadow me."

My skin is beautiful; not damaged,
just not light like hers.
We could be two tones of the same earth,
two tastes of the same dessert.

"Self, shadow me."

I have a mind that is not hers,
eyes that see so well from my exclusive vantage.

"Self, shadow me."

I keep my midnight black eye shadow,
to acknowledge the seriousness of my contempt,
honor my resentment,
and my indignance.
I receive every stroke of sparkling darkness with
gentle respect,

before my sadness can even begin to lose its hold,
flake away.

"Self, shadow me."

I am made from deep golden honey,
and she from inside rich earthy almonds.
We glow separately,
together.

The Suitcase

The suitcase always smells like India.
Sandalwood? Talcum powder?
That distinct from-India smell.

My parents collected their memories of India 1975,
locked them up into a rectangle shape,
which they carried into the walk-in closet
of their main bedroom in America.

I was raised in a house that stole time.
Made out like a bandit, relishing all the old ways,
just the same as all my friends' homes.
An entire community marches forward to an
old drumbeat.
Even if India grows to 70 years of independence,
and hatches its own MTV generation,
we are happy to dance to 1975.

Time does freeze.

I once met a woman who I could have been if I never left India.
She couldn't comprehend
why I refused wear anything but plain traditional clothes
when I visited my mother country,
and why I knew so much of the meaning in my traditions,
more than she did.
She—high heels, leather miniskirt, even a boyfriend at
her side.

Me—feet firmly planted on this calendar with pages
still stuck,
smelling of India 1975.

My body is a living, breathing time capsule.

Sparking Bay

Fresh peaches undress themselves on my tongue
from inside my white glass of Riesling.
Lemons unleash teasing bites upon me,
from a once frozen place in the sorbet of time.

Sailboats sit perfectly still, paying homage to an incredible
collaborator, the sparking bay.
It is certainly the August sun melting my worries away;
but it feels like the water is blanketing me and him from
feeling any sort of winter.

It could have been a dream,
but I can **never erase the small traces of tundra he makes**
with his lips. His word-attack builds swiftly from an
arsenal of syllable-by-syllable bullets
You. should. take. more. care. of. your. looks.
I submerge into a dark frigid cold,
where sharp icicles take hold
and pierce my skin.

Instead of slicing my day with the blade of his sentence,
I let the fury have its say—letting hot words burst
from my throat in the privacy of my home,
clearing my mind's calendar, making it summer again,
so his words won't freeze me for days upon years to come.

I break things off with my excusing thoughts,
realizing HE DOES NOT OWN ME,
I OWN MY CHOICES, THIS IS MY BODY!

I stride closer to my strength, my innate Beauty.
I let my potent anger clear my mind,
purging the trash he recklessly
polluted into our glorious day,
exposing his gloom.

I exhale,
march down my own aisle with orange blossoms.
to renew my vows with the sun,
letting her warmth kiss my cheeks.

The thing about summer—
She needs you to keep choosing her.

Carousel, a Poem about Communication

I am stuck on a loud carousel,
blaring tedious pretend-happy music.
Mystified by when the coin was ever put in,
making it all go around and around.

I am irritated by a rude fellow rider, staring creepily,
grinning as if I have the answer to every single thing.

I sit on a horse who never put its foot down,
blaming you for not knowing the important things,
my heart's desires.
Hating you for forgetting me in plain sight.

Wondering why you always wore that plastered-on
concerned face,
why you wouldn't turn off the ride,
and let me get down.

As I turn the circle for the 100th or 200th time,
I see in the passing mirror,
that I am the one with the goofy made-up smile.

I was the one **sitting on a flying horse,**
refusing to touch the earth,
wishing so hard
that you could read my loud mind. (Why can't you?)
refusing to accept that your ears are all the way over there
in your chair. (Why are you so far?)
I am the one refusing to listen to my desires, my needs,

and state them out loud in the open in a complete sentence.
I never take life's great dare to speak my real fears.

My fury finally blasts out from hiding
inside my mind's parenthesis—
SERIOUSLY, WHY CAN'T YOU HEAR MY THOUGHTS?!

I scream until I crack the passing mirror,
until my horse collapses, until the only sound left is
my clear voice, and my sanity.

It turns out, I was the one in the operator's booth all along.
I always had the keys.

Not Roses, a New Phase of an Old Friendship

Sometimes it's not roses or rainbows.
Sometimes the friendship isn't so thick and buttery
just watery.
Not even water, sometimes just vapors

of **nostalgia dressed up as hope,**
but still smell of moldy grief,
the pungent kind of a friend who stops showing up.

Sometimes I don't want to giggle and smile,
and reflect on the flowery times we had for years.
I've shed my last tear,
but the picture from my window stays the same,
replaying in my brain:
she doesn't come back.

I want to mince the book of friendship
we wrote together.
my lines in blood promises,
hers in disappearing ink.

Sometimes I want to eat a whole cake
to numb the hurt, and
never share it.
Ever.
Again.

Instead of words like
This is temporary or

I'll brighten up and buy some roses or
This is more than fine, I need to learn to be independent,
I prefer the single word:
Cunt.

If I don't utter the truth for myself,
my anger remains my vanilla-frosted poison,
deteriorating my organs, leaving me wondering,
Why is my energy running so low?
And why are there never enough cupcakes?

A Place for Anger

I turn my anger into thread,
barely visible, secure, undeniable.
Carefully, I pull its unyielding strength through my needle
intentionally, like a ritual.

My anger is a best friend whose pinky swear I wrap
around my finger because she claims
I matter. I am worth fighting for.

I stitch it into the fabric of my every day,
into the firm words I say. when I state my needs.
If she is loud in my head,
it is because her fabric was ripped,
a necessity gone unmet, unrequested.
Any loose ends eventually find their way
into my material,
solidifying the seams of my sentences,
weaving a firm pathway to my dreams.

If I let anger's needle pierce my day,
then she gives me my vocabulary of *No*,
ensures I am not eaten alive,
refuses anything that doesn't protect me.

She provides me shape,
containment, safety,
place.

Song of Revolution

I will rain down on parades if I must.
I will rain, I will pour, I will storm,
I will thunder.

I will rain down on your parade—
that army of thoughts.
Your judgement marches loudly,
but I will say *No.*
Elegantly, Decisively, Irrevocably,
No.
I will not say yes because guilt takes
a ride on my shoulders.
I will say *No.*

Here it is one last time,
for those of you who didn't believe me:

I will rain down on entire parades—
on your parade, if I must.

And, I must.

She Stole my Dream

She took the heat from underneath my breath,
that space where words warm up
before they realize themselves.
She stole my entire trajectory,
carved out the very patterns
my footprints were supposed to make.
She landed in a chair that was made for me.

She stole my dream.

She ransacked the kitchen where I transform,
took every ingredient from my fridge, every substance
from my cabinets,
let all of my water boil off.

But **I was the one**

who cast her as a crook.
All along, I was the bandit,
stole my own hours, my own days.
She was never the guilty party.

I collect what I stole, what was mine already.
I dig for cobwebbed caskets of buried poems,
excavate my heart I left throbbing on a dance
floor somewhere.

Equipped with a supply of oxygen,
my own love on my back,

I reach deep into a black ocean,
make contact with manatee-shaped fears,
wrestle with my friendly monsters.
With sheer force, gumption, and every pound of joy—
I am at once defeated, at once victorious,
at once bloody, at once nurtured,
thrown into an excruciating ecstasy.

There was always enough ocean for all of us.

Heroine's Journey Chapter 4:

Finding the Favor of Success

This chapter of our Heroine's Journey is the last step of the traditional Hero's Journey, where our main character wins against various challenges by emerging a changed and strengthened person. She arrives to a clear sense of *what* she is in the world.

This is my celebration chapter. The poems here arise after resolving the initial challenges of working as a woman in a man's world and achieving a state of success. There is a clear sense of victory satisfaction, and achievement.

Pour the Vodka

Be a pirate —
steal time from your own ship
to make an exuberant sparkling noise.

Celebrate yourself,
shut everything down
to remember that you are a force.

Your vessel is running on your power,
it is going strong,
so stop and rob your own time.

Pour the vodka,
make a raucous.

It may feel like you're stealing time,
but you're opening it up
to cheer for your own winnings.

You are inflating your heart, not your head.
filling yourself with your own buoyancy,
elevating everyone else in your wake.

Raise a glass!
But put down your ifs, ands, and buts.
You know the ones:
I'm happy, but it's just my job.
I'm happy, and it wasn't that hard, this is embarrassing.
I'm happy, still what if I could have done better?

Let that discomfort sink in a little too,
as the congratulations flow
down your throat,
lest the celebrations feed your weeds,
amplifying every doubt.
instead of sustaining your self-esteem, your impact on
this world.

Do not say your thanks as if it were just polite conversation.
You are clinking your glass to change
the very quality of time.
It is your chance to drink in the light
of your own sunshine.

If you glance up to the painting
that is the sky,
you'll see how the gods have already decorated.
They are ready for you
to make your hoopla.
Waiting for you
to make a raucous.

Artist with a Day Job

I spend my days walking in grids,
mechanically crossing cubicle intersections,
shepherding a chaos of information
into order,
so pointed decisions can be made,
like the right angles in which I step.
I gain altitude by siphoning specifics, distilling details.
patterning a process that works like it should,
engineering some movement forward.

At night,
I never rest.

Instead, I listen for beauty in the opposite direction:
taking the facts of reality—
the splash of morning in my coffee creamer,
the squint of my eyes at high noon,
evening's slower rhythm, and night's special glow.
Mix it together without any notion of sequence,
throwing out the diagram.
Swirl together all the days of the week,
cut apart different months into strange shapes with the
craft scissors of my intuition,
usher distant particulars to compress close together,
until they become a new seed.

I add rainwater which is my fresh-squeezed desire,
the sweat of my attention, a scoop of Miracle Grow(™),

extra dirt I collect breaking down mountains of standards
and rules,
a love so messy
anything fresh might emerge,
maybe in neon green.

Every single element destined never to return to its
first form,
transcending into something new.
Never again to be the same.

Be Well

Sunflowers grow in the sun.
Don't mistake
the bitter olives
as hating life,
they grow out of
happiness too.
Even the winter root vegetables,
beets and potatoes,
are grown out with extreme joy,
stretch marks on the earth where they emerge
splitting open for new life,
a welcome abundance.

When my heart is in full harvest,
I live in infinite prism form,
in full color.

Van Gogh
could not find a sunflower or touch
a canvas in the worst of his illness,
imprisoning his own heart, his whole soul,
and all of his art.

If you make any effort,
may it always be to follow your own sun,
imagine your full bloom,
let your petals extend and enjoy the breeze.
Be heartful, be creative,
and most of all—
be well.

Run to my Victories

Sometimes my thoughts come together swiftly.
My words want to run to their sentences,
and my sentences want to sit in my lap.

On these bright breezy days,
I rest in the cozy space between
two   words,
sprawl out and lusciously lay on the bed between two

paragraphs, and I peel myself back in the dressing rooms
that emerge at the end of every story,

to see how I come back together again.

On other days,
my cloudy thoughts stubbornly hold back.
I have to tune in so hard
to hear the conversation
the
rain
makes
with
the
lake, and write down every word,
scribbling down every scrap
made from the fabric of truth.

I listen,
so **I can dance in a dress stitched in poetry**
and run to my victories.

The Secret of Friendship

May we reflect each other
in **the lazy summer river of our wide-open souls,**
seeing ourselves in each other in spite of bumpy
rocks and dicey falls along the way.

Each of us floating easily,
without expectation,
softly tugged along
deeper into our own lives.

It is the secret of friendship—
inside the soft droplets of gentleness,
within the cool clear pools of honesty,
there is immense power.

Enough to deliver us slowly from a river
into our promising ocean,
that place we most desire,
to where we were heading all along.

Bamboo

My summertime shadow
walks alongside me.

She is my long-time friend,
my chatty close cousin named fear.

Still, I am a far-reaching bamboo tree,
gunning for the sun.

Straight to Her Destiny

Was it inside the tiara on top of her head,
or in the last stroke of blush on her cheek,
or in the shine of his shoes?
Was it in the orange lights of the party
or inside the red streamers?
Where did this deluge of belief begin?

It is hard to say where this undeniable shower
of love came from,
but the bride floated up so high on her chariot,
straight to her destiny. It's still a mystery
how she lifted the rest of us.

I sat still in my chair, moved beyond the touch of my feet
to the ground.
Maybe it was in the ocean that kissed the shore outside.
It was everywhere, this new profound feeling that
true love
is right in front of me for my taking.
Was it in the perfect candy on top of the perfect cupcakes?

A wedding, though, is never made of these things.
It happened like this:
Before this moment came, she conjured it by surrendering
to her friend already in front of her.

She stopped wishing for a grand device,
toppled over the tall forts around her,
stepped onto her wide-open field.

By her wedding day, her heart was so awake, so fragile,
even the clouds felt it and **they broke wide open,**
made us all drunk with love.
Making a trio of friends promise to never settle
for anything less than an extraordinary capital L love,
filled with ordinary everyday lowercase r respect.

The favor of the rain came down and made me
switch my hands from praying
for love, to separating them, resting them on my chest.
I am the one who has to lift the doors first.

True love was etched in my skin like a blessing,
so I don't have to conjure a single thing.
Love is more than possible, it is inevitable, it is already
inside of me.
I want to run up to the clouds, and rip open my own sky
so I can fall, and fall, and fall like the rain did that day,
in love.

Watery Body

I can build an entire house out of all the letters.
Two stories—mine and the one told
by my watery body, reflected back onto me by the lake.
The first story is of curiosity, written by my first glance
into the water, noticing a familiar shape,
I peer closer, listen harder to her account back to me,
the one of belonging.
I lean in
all the way.

Washed by my own body, I glide back and forth
like he did inside of me that day.
Empowered as a woman, lost my alphabet—the old order
of things—my virginity.
I wrote my first sentence as a woman that day.
Soaked in my own reflection.
Dove in, straight for myself.

The Elevation of Sex

Can we please talk about
How. Much. I. Love. Sex.?
But it was a total and complete surprise,
like an unexpected holiday.
Holy everything,
where did this even come from?

Here's how it went:

Suddenly, he is a volcano so bold to me,
lava to touch, molten rock to taste.
I love it when he erupts in me.

Eyes so devastating, two ocean waves that lift me up
and bring the very end to me.
He licks the leather on my boots (what!), I am moved
by him.
I dismiss my brain and its cargo of lingo,
I let his ship navigate me somewhere else.

We always kiss like there's no yesterday.
No politics in the bedroom otherwise
we'd be in a hell—divided.
He touches my map and he never gets lost in me.

My body keeps talking to him, speaking brand new
languages. I am frightened
by my instant fluency.
My body is speaking languages of the world's lovers—

Turkish, Hindi, Spanish, French, Burmese, Greek:

Seni istiyorum
Muze tum chahiye
Te *Deseo*
Je te veux
Mainn ko lohkyintaal
Se thélo

My body says things that I could never think.
I leap onto him
easily,
acrobatics on the couch
I never even choreographed.
I am summoned into a new foreign place,
deeply impossibly familiar.
ten thousand suns may rise all at the same time, but they
can't
compete.
He leaves me thirsty.

But how?

I used to think between-the-sheets was probably
a chore to complete.
I didn't know I had this secret climate, this lush desire,
my own potency to generate
heat.
Instantly I am both the flame and flammable.

Fire ignites when I see his sexy jeans,
they command me onto him.
His tempting words melt my ears.
I'm not an actress yet.
I am suddenly a sultry school chica with fishnet legs,
role-playing like I never knew how not to.
I am astounded, it makes me laugh out loud
on top of the bed.

Sticky sweet, lick it all off to see what's next on the menu.
He doesn't just please me, he eases me into his breakfast.
Like hot crepes off a pan,
I can hear him sizzlin' sugar in me.
He just sits close to me, and my stovetop starts burning
so he can cook in me.

How is this happening?
Is it him?

He is so hot to me,
lava to touch.

Is it me?

I am molten rock
to taste.

Don't, don't, don't
cool me down yet.

Feast Well

Feast well
on only the loving things.

Bite into life's pomegranate whole,
never settle
for insufficient seeds.

Let all the extra love
spill
down
your cheeks.

Now that Kamala will be VP (Previously published in Brown Girl Magazine on Jan 20, 2021)

I used to wish that I were white
and that I could wipe
away the dirt from my skin,
because I didn't fit in.
Sure, I can serve you Indian food,
but when the smell becomes too much,
I know how to pack it back in,
expertly dicing up my Indianness before letting it all out.

When you pull up a seat at the table for me,
I won't get comfortable.
You may ask me to teach you something
as if I were a visiting lecturer,
or play show and tell, so I must explain myself
and then put it all away after the game is done.

These chairs you named for me
were never designed for me.
Like a game of musical chairs,
your fast songs will start again,
so I race for a new place somewhere,
carrying around all my stuff.

Now that Kamala will be VP,
the White House will have someone who looks like me.
She will see her reflection, and always see the color brown.
Now when people ask me, *Where are you from, originally?*

I can think of that White House mirror instead.
I am a part of the American equation.
Inclusion is not selected stories boxed up like pretty saris,
that you can ooh and aah over.
My skin is no longer a marketing campaign
seeking out buyers,
when the truth is I grew up in Jersey.

Now when you pull up a chair, I can take my shoes off,
put down my bags, bring the whole Taj Mahal to the table.
Soon, we will dissolve your table all together,
and sit on life's richer floors,
where earth's gravity will center us
like never before.

Song of Construction

My life is a house I must endure.

Its couches are sagging, crumpling me down.
The floors are too flimsy for my weight.
The walls are so thin, they echo with
Other People's Thoughts.

Ceilings so short I have to act small.
My windows won't open:
I can't breathe.

I stop
to write a peace treaty with my space,
inscribe amendments that put my desires
on the dining room table,
strikethrough clauses where fear was my architect.

Every word I write adds an inch to my ceiling, and I can
be big.
Every honest sentence
strengthens my floorboards so I can
          dance wildly.
And my walls, oh my walls. They sing
beautiful sounds
that nuzzle my ears,
sounds so familiar: my own voice.

My pen draws windows that open to the breeze,
I can feel the crackle of rustling leaves making their way to fly.
Every question mark I write - *Where am I going?*
What do I want to do before I die?
What does it feel like? Really?
adds new feathers to my couch,
I can unfold, stretch, and unfurl.

I lavish my life's ink,
surrender to my heart's accord
until the air in my kitchen is a fresh fall morning.
until acorns find themselves at my doorstep,
looking for a good place to grow
together with me.

Heroine's Journey Chapter 5

Awakening to a Sense of Spiritual Aridity

Despite the success that she has achieved, our Heroine has difficulty getting up out of bed. She has suppressed many of her emotions to create the success that she assumed was the pathway to happiness and fulfillment. She feels betrayed, as her energy for pushing forward in all the "right" ways has led her to her own spiritual aridity.

My poetry from this section is about facing realities and taking a high-level look under the hood. It is the preparation stage for my need to dive deeper.

Out of Bed

There is no prize for the person
who suffers the most.

Majestic rainbows appear,
whether or not you
endure your mind's hailstorms.

So, welcome yourself
out of bed.

Trade in the tired creases of your sheets
and the flattened pillows of your crisis committee,
for a cup of morning air,

where the sun is situated
above your head
like a crown,

where your feet touch down
upon this day's territory like royalty,

well before your own brain
pours down rain,
weighing down your mattress,
soaking bad weather into
the whole day.

What Was Your Day Like?

Tell me, what was your day like?
What was your day like?
Did you hear and did you listen?
Did you tell yourself the truth?
Did you speak it out loud?

Did you listen to yourself,
or did you listen to everyone else
and let them hold all your weapons,
so they can erase your thoughts from your tongue,
before you gave yourself a chance to speak,
a moment to be heard,
never sending your choices into your world,
letting their words be your white-out,
marking yourself blank, to be written on top of
and scribbled all over?

What was your day like?
Did you run and hide
in a hole like a mole inside of your skin?
All over again, another time?
Burying yourself deeply until you don't breathe,
and then you wonder
why some words you don't even recognize
are spit out of your head,
instead of letting the loud truth in your heart
shine its way through and out?

Or did you
...look inside?
Did you take a second to inhale?
Did you soften your eyes?

Did you ask yourself these questions:
-How do I feel?
-What do I know is for real?
-Real real?
-What do I need?
-What do I need?

Did you take another breath?
Did you listen to your feet?
Did you listen to your heart?
Did you look inside your throat,
where the words sometimes get stuck
in fear they'll hurt someone else?
What are those words?
What was your day like?
What was your day like?
Did you listen so hard? To your heart?
Did you hear your cells
say what they need to say?
Did you speak them out loud into the cold air,
or the hot air, whispering them inside the heat
of your mouth?
You don't even need a key to open up that door.

What was your day like?
Did you listen to your heart?
What did you hear?
Did you get to see your day light?
Did you get to see your day light?
What was your day like?

My Career as Pizza

Instead of giving my thanks before dinner,
I take a moment to look
at my plate of food.

I offer myself sustenance from the warm soup
of my family,
a savory quiche appetizer of hearty
vacations with good friends,
the cupcakes of love from my nieces and nephew,
all upon gorgeous tableware that matches my heart.

Still, the bland dish
of my work life leaves me hungry for more.

I claim my worth, and
I desire to use it for good,
I need to translate the force of my being into impact.

I crave a deep-dish pizza life,
but make the most with the casserole in front of me,
pretending to be moved by the herbs and
spices I keep piling on.

I deserve to be fed
a more fulfilling meal.

I make room on my plate
to dream up a well-nourished life.

Just. Have. Fun.

It all came tumbling down,
our epic sky-high plan to

Just.
Have.
Fun.

It all came tumbling down
when **you midwifed a new poem from me.**

I felt richly connected, yet
our link was never meant to be
fastened.

It was destined to vanish,
like the verse I uttered in your presence,
but never penned into ink,
doomed to disappear.

Now I'm left
to midwife myself from me.

Leap of Faith

I didn't know that things like
diving into the great unknown,
following my dreams,
taking a leap of faith

also meant
plunging into my dismay,
the place where ghosts of dreams-not-followed
hang together.

These skeletons
don't let you skip by their table,
they stop you in your tracks,
pour you a drink,
trance you into having a seat.

I assess if they are vicious,
making me sit in this shit made of grief,
so merciless, slowing me down when I
should be speeding up to live
the life of my dreams.

But they are benevolent, **giving me**
space to remember
the spells they cast on themselves.

I listen to their songs of despair,
even dance with them,
weep as I accept their bitter drinks,
giggle, and even laugh a little.

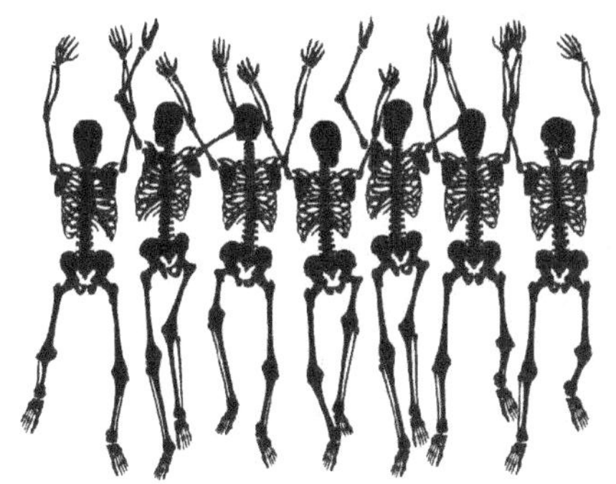

Invisible, Nobody

Sometimes I wonder how the wind
lives her life.

She's invisible, nobody can photograph her,
pay her attention.
She is apparent only in things outside of herself—
a tree's rustling leaves, my hair changing direction,
someone's hat flying off in a new choreography.

Luckily, I don't have to wonder.
The wind sat down next to me
just to tell me she's happy that nobody sees her
because nobody casts their wishes upon her,

asks her to smile
asks her to go left when she wants to go right,
asks her to wear a tight dress,
asks her to wear a looser dress,
asks her to wear a different color,
asks her to change her filter,
be taller, be bigger, stand up, don't stand too tall,
be comfortable.

***I am free to frown*, she says.**

Free to absorb her own discomfort
and disappointment.
Doesn't worry if her anger turns someone's umbrella
inside out,

she can't help it that she moves
through her truth.

I love my ease, she says.

Then she flew away with her clear ethereal wisdom.
Or maybe not, maybe she's sitting right here
always next to me,
letting me be.

I want you to breathe, she says.

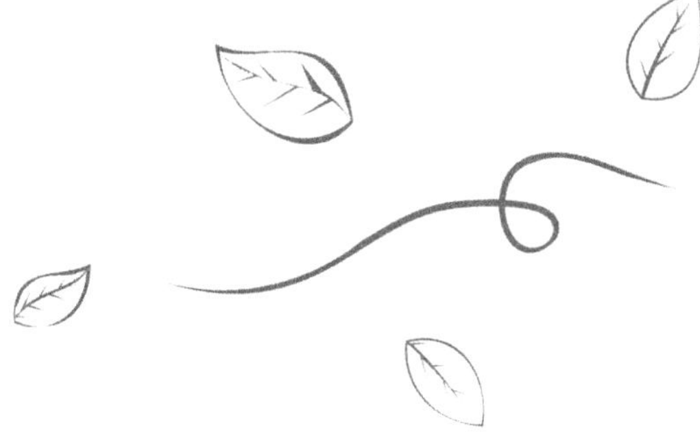

Permission to Grieve

Even the weeping willow is growing
taller, stronger, drinking in
her share of the sun.

Loose Ends

If I could tie the sheets together in knots,
I would.
Then you could climb out
from your sheer absence, your unavailability.
But time has no fabric,
some loose ends are never meant to tie
together.

I am letting you go,
your body, my image of you.
I tear apart the love story I cast you into,
setting my soul's Taj Mahal on fire,
burning away every thread of material.

But never your memory.
I put us into a rice paper box
so we can see through it
with soft, even blurred vision,
whenever we want to.

I plant two seeds—
one for you and one for me
so we can feel our separation.
We reaped.
We sowed.
Now an empty field
lays full
of gratitude.

Extra Dallop of Love, Song of Self-Esteem

I felt exhausted
before the party started.

Cooking up a storm of approval,
a long table of meals,
just to earn my keep.

Building walls and walls of garam masala and
tadka daal, sharing it all,
keeping nothing
but bitter insanity.

Scared of exposing my pungent anger,
my over-salted sadness,
oily shame, and
steaming hot love.

I spiced the food instead of polluting
your air with my inner textures.
My kitchen was a panic room—pouring insecurities
into an oven, just to bake them in.

Serving plate upon plates in exchange
for your closeness.
My contribution, a payment,
for a spoonful of your affinity.

My afterparty was confusion
about if I secured anything in return,

whether I ever felt fed,
or if I was empty, still hungry for something.

I left out the important stash,
my intimacy.

Before having you over for dinner,
I will now stock up my heart first,
and clean a different kind of kitchen,
the place I cook up the ways I show up.
On my personal stove, I lift the lid, notice any insecurity,
let its steam trace my face.
Then **I fill up on my own rich love,**
silky gratitude, self-nutrition.
I help myself to an extra dollop
of my friends' love, my family's familiarity.

Before inviting anyone in,
I make contact first
with the flavors bursting inside of me.

Skin of a Stranger

Please always remember me.
That is my inner motivation, my subtext, my forever
demand of whomever stands in front of me.

My Uber driver said it is the human condition
to forget;
It's why we take tests, he said.

Still, I spill potion into the air to make you think of me,
cast every spell I can think to speak,
try to brand myself so hotly, deeply inside your mind,
so you never forget.

These are bold attempts
to work against
nature's tides.
After all, **we are all one of the masses.**

Maybe I was never afraid of being forgotten,
but terrified of one day touching my own arm,
and feeling the skin of a stranger.
Catching myself in a car window
and not recognizing the eyes
that look back.

The Meditation Poem I Didn't Write

I didn't write the meditation poem today.
I let myself get consumed by a wind tunnel made of
spinning anger
and nauseating regret.
I let sadness have the driver's seat and take me to

it-doesn't-matter-where, it's not where I wanted to go.
I let the world's great problems steal my show,
and my sanity.

I refused to write that poem,
the one about rescue, where **I drop myself a rope ladder**
made of my own breath.

Burn the List

On my way out,
in the hallway mirror, I say
You're not the fixer upper,
you're the dream house,
wiggle into your vastness.

On the front patio,
I pour myself a glass of pleasure,
and a plate of fortitude.

When I start with my wholeness,
I stop my preambles of
I think…
or
I don't know if I'm saying this right…
or
Tell me if this makes sense…

I am not broken,
not in shambles.
I am not a project that seeks an end.
I am a place to begin.

Burn the list,
there's nothing to fix.

I know what I wish
to speak.

I am infinity—
swooping in and out in **constructive compassion for myself.**
My mind is sane, my body is a miracle.
I look up to see myself in my best light.
I am the brightness of a pink moon.

My Anger: Poison, Prayer or Ally?

Anger is inside of me,
what will I do with her fever?

Will I let my worthy rage become
my poison, my prayer or my ally?

Poison
If I am ashamed of my anger and call her
ugly,
she is pressed inside, left
to feast on my own guts,
my own brain.

My voiceless scream runs sharp
through my veins, which become a hotbed
for my bacterial shame
while I whisper to the world
my too-polite words.

Prayer
I build a chimney to let the rage out,
let it slay the air outside of me
instead of letting it eat me.
I am still so
ashamed
of how it looks.
Does it make me look mean?
Does it make me look ungrateful?
Does it make me the angry person of my nightmares?

I snuff her when she's halfway out
practically swallowing my own vomit.

My rage believes in herself,
her own gory truths,
her own blood red beauty,
her own glory.
She persists and persists,
like a prayer, waiting to be
witnessed.

Ally
When I let my anger have her say,
she fights viciously for my safety. She says:
I am not going to take it lying down!

She points me straight
to my unmet needs
so I can bid for them clearly, but only after
she has fully released from me.

She always holds a spot for me,
my place in this world,
the ground upon which I can always land.
If my rage is fighting and fighting
for my life's very territory,
then she is my brilliant ally.

Not Guilty

After two-decades of nothing
but a blustery winter,
having proclaimed myself guilty,

Not guilty is children shrieking in delight with full lungs,
racing into a warm, welcoming sea.

Not guilty is a graceful shower of blushing
pink cherry blossom petals, giving thanks to themselves
for forgiveness.

But not the white petals.
They remain repenting forever,
refusing any color.

Not guilty is the satisfaction of rest
after yesterday's traffic jams in my brain are banished
so far away from the present moment,
further than a distant memory,
further even than a previous life,
further even more, prior to Pangea,
when there was only stardust in the air,
if that.

Not guilty is relaxing my tight hands

from my strangled throat,
releasing them palms up,
asking out loud for my well-deserved blessings.
Deserving like a baby deserves her first milk.

Deserving.
Deserving.
Deserving.

Not guilty.
Not guilty.
Not guilty.

Not guilty is inviting pleasure, dancing
continuously.
I can easily be a brightly lit
living prayer.

That's Not Where it Hurts

When I confess I'm hurting,
please know my heart is at risk of cementing shut,
probably already crushed.

I can say, They ignored my request.
You can say, *Fuck the patriarchy.*
I want to advocate for my soul
and reply with a prayer to myself that goes:
Thank you, but that's not where it hurts.

Sit with me in silence
for a few more beats.
This extra space between words
is the invisible material
from which we build a magic bench together,
made from our sheer presence.

I can say, I'm ashamed of how I feel.
You can say, *There's nothing to be ashamed of. Being a*
woman
isn't a fault.
I spin my prayer beads one more time. *Thank you, but*
that's not where it hurts.

Let's keep making that bench from our breath,

so we can both sit in a place where
we can break out of our skin.

I feel scared, I feel unsafe. I feel vulnerable
every morning. And all I need
is your warm heart to keep exhaling space into this bench.

We can smell the roses soon
but only if I can see the roots first,
let the sludge of it spill
into our sight.

Together we can find,
exactly
where it hurts, what must
be aired, very slowly.

From this bench we make together, my shame
stops clouding up my view.
I can finally see your nourishing eyes,
the green grass, and the happy trees around us.

Thank you, but that's not where it hurts is my invitation

to shape a sturdy, quieter bench
upon which our friendship lives,
a prayer that can only be sung together.

Custom Tailored

I don't have a direct feed to all the treasures in the world.
So when my daughter asks for a new toy,
my shame is gaping,
like the rips in her old doll's dress.

How can she know her happiness,
if I can't show her mine?

How can I know joy if I never accept the sting
of shame's death stare?
Claim its custom-tailored laser
lacerations to my heart's fabric?
My personal shame fits like a made-to-measure suit,
how could anyone else understand it?

I dare myself to say, *I feel ashamed*
to a trusted friend. *Saying no*
to my daughter
is saying
I am not man enough.

I kill shame's power source, slowly dismantling the atoms
from its steam pressure force by taking it out from hiding,
from its lonely house of despair.

I drape my grief in the silence between us,
letting it drip, airing it out
in the foyer of my soul, where I enter into my choice,
deciding for myself:

I am man enough, fully stocked with virility,
opening the door for possibility,
for a richer story. Maybe it was never
about being a man, as if a man can ever be a thing,
like a tie or a suit.
What if the story was always only about
my becoming?

Riot

I'm the middlest.

Middle child: I never knew where I stood
The ground below was in constant flux,
depending on who I was with.

I signed external constitutions
to determine my bylaws,
putting them on like paper dresses,
pacifying other people's wars
even if mine was just getting started.

My internal rumble was a just a tiny whisper,
hoping to break my own voice free
from the noise inside my crowded head.

Never understood where I started, where others ended.
Slipping on people's shoes so comfortably,
walking the world in silent crisis.

I only had to look at my two feet
to know I was already here in plain sight,
rooted irrevocably into my own life.

I make my own riot
by breathing deeply,
slowly filling up
with the divinity above me,
below me, all around,

until I am at full buoyancy.
It is not crowded anymore.
I'm the only one who lives here.

I keep the light on for myself,
in case I wander away.

Meet Me in the Middle

Why don't you meet me
in the middle?

I'll make us each
a royal crown to remind us that
this awkward place
is where the majestic trumpets
always play,
celebrating the always choppy voyages
for true understanding.

Some stay too polite,
not ready to roll up their pant legs,
get their feet splotched in the mud.

Don't worry, I'll be there too;
my feet are already goopy.
It's only disgusting if we say it is.

Thank you for stepping into it
with me—that conversation
made of stilted words like *When you say that, it*
feels like you are bored of me.
weirder words have never spilled out from me,
so different than the conversation
I scripted in my brain.

I dare you. What if you confess what my presence does
to you?

It takes practice talking out of a mouth
too numb from niceties,
but ready to be a little risky.

If we speak through our reservoir of discomfort,
we enrich the soil of our friendship,
and **our kinship to all the wild**
things in the world.

But it is terrifying. What if I slip and land on my back?
And what if that frightens you away?
It is horrifying. *What if my rage actually-actually kills you?*
I mean I could...
Wait, am I, could I be a murderer?
It is appalling. *What if it kills...us?*

Still, the only substitute is a manicured front yard,
a picket fence of practiced sentences separating
me from

you.

I wish to take notice of what is happening
inside my breath, mind, my guts,
and bare the messy truth.

If you don't take this invitation,
our exchanges remain our shields
of well-rehearsed stories, casual comebacks:
I'm fine, great. Did I tell you that crazy story about
the time...
or
Yes, things are not the same, but I'm counting my blessings!
skilled in entertaining,
missing the more adventurous landing all together.

Why don't you meet me in the muck?
Let's make a deal:
if either of us starts to wipe off the mud,
puts our good shoes back on,
let's ask a tender question, delicately:
        I just wonder...what it would be like,
        if you...just said...what...you were thinking?
Invite
the
other
back
slowly,
carefully
into
love's
daunting sludge.

If it's not awkward,
it's not living.

Meet me in the middle,
where your jaw releases
guilelessly,
where the only agenda is to
connect,
the only intention is to
witness.
The only hopes are to
see and be seen.

Meet me in the middle,
where your heart might race a lot,
where all the love is free
to ooze, to speak,
to be.

I am a Bottom Feeding Fish

I am sometimes a bottom feeding fish:
slimy, green with envy
dripping negativity,
screeching out my familiar tracks:
Why him and not me?
Congratu-fuckin-lations.
I hope she messes up.

I fantasize a momentary glee
like a sugar rush.
In my thoughts, I am sticking out my foot
so they trip on their way up.

My green-eyed-monster
may seem slimy and green,
stink like moldy seaweed.

But I am
not disgusting.

My bitterness was never the crazy
auntie I lock up in the attic;
It is only the closed door
that makes her unhinged.

I ask my envy what she is hungry for,
how much will be enough.
to feed her

Her words open me to the next part of my ocean,
the next juncture in my vast adventures.
Sometimes, I even thank her.

The Danger of Vulnerability (aka What Rude People Call Intimacy Issues)

I don't trust you.
What if you gut the insides from me?
What if you steal my property, the living
breathing estate of everything I make?
What if you drain my water fountain,
where all my ideas are born like minnows
asking to be freed?

I don't trust you.
You might saw off the center of *my* being,
replace it with *your* mission control,
steering me, accelerating me, into
a CR. AAASH
LANDDDI
NG.

I don't trust you.
What if I need you? What if I hitchhike into my life,
with a soft thumb exposed,
and you run me over with your fucking truck,
wipe me out before even asking
where I was heading?

What if you see blood
all over my lips
from the scavenging I have done?
What if you rip out my teeth after I am done talking,

and I fold my mouth forever in defeat?
I mean what do you care,
if I vanished off your
earth?
Would you just turn the dial on your music box again,
waiting for your next
tomorrow to pop,
the one without any fragrance of me?

Still, I don't want to miss out on your generous
landing pad,
where I could even build myself
a new house

but first
we'll have to lay out all my organs and maybe yours too
on the table,
then frame them
in my vomit.

Can the sun in your heart
contain it, to see my biggest fall,
my bike's handlebars and my brain all splattered on the
ground
like a small bird no longer sitting in traffic?
Can the sun in my heart handle it if you come to the scene
without your ambulance, carrying no medicine,
just a bag of your mushy gushy love?

I don't want to need you.
It's easier to throw our talks onto the ground,
burn them, turn around, blink my eyes,
step away,
never
see you
again.

What if I let you see me though,
and then I am no longer an interesting story,
just a blob pulsing, eating, and shitting?
Then you'll know.

Then you'll go.

Let's make a new contract:
I don't want you to eat me.
I don't want you to take my voice,
like certain men take from women.
Like certain mothers take from children.
Like certain fathers take from futures.
I would rather just dip my toes into our pool.
My flip flops are completely within reach.
I still have my towel on,
I prefer not to get my hair all wet
than risk losing my throat, my neck, my esophagus,
my oxygen.
My fear comes out in four words:
Fuck. You. Organ. Thief.

In some other undersea language, it might come out as these three: *Please don't leave.*

Heroine's Journey Chapter 6: Initiation and Descent to the Goddess, Diving into her Underworld of Shadows

In this chapter, the Heroine is faced with a life-changing event that transforms her irreversibly and causes her to plunge fully into her darker feelings to find her own truth.

The poetry here is from life's chasms that can drop me to my soul's basement, from where I can see my own source. Specifically, it is an experience in my past of sexual assault in the workplace that I now see is not something that happened "to" me, but rather an event that happened "for" me. If not for it, I would not have learned to speak from my core and determine my own path.

The greatest focus in this entire book is accepting and honoring the messy middle of life. If there is a such thing as dancing in rubble, it happens most intentionally in this chapter. Here you will find many such reflections from when I reach down and sit with my discomfort until I increasingly make more space to allow for all the complexities. It is not that I become "stronger," it is that I become vaster. Specifically, in this section, I describe my process of transitioning from "managing" my shame and rage into the place of allowing it, experiencing it, and letting it have its full expression, which makes more space for love and peace.

Be a Warrior

Be a warrior.
Be the first to walk into the dust-up
of life's confusion.

Be the first to march into the muck
of your sadness.

There is hope
inside of the hardest
terrains.

Be a warrior.
Bite straight into the overripe
fruit of your feelings gone
unseen too long.

Venture into the places that are unknown,
where you have more questions than answers.

Be a warrior.
March into tension
with eyes wide open, slow down your breathing,
bringing every nuance into light.
Your weaponry is your massive
curiosity.

Go in barefoot,
expose the soft center

of every place you've walked,
vulnerable, ready to receive the heartbeat
from the earth.

Room to Grieve, the Swamps of New Orleans

In the soupy swamps of New Orleans, we wise trees
tune into sadness.

Some call our land dirty, muddy,
disgusting even.
Those who do always face away,
scared of being eaten by dark crocodiles,
afraid of being bitten by
depression, swallowed into
a permanent despondency.

We trees are happy to sit
with every dense pile of sorrow you bring for us.
The entire swamp is waiting for you, in case
you want to **pour out some of your golden**
grief.

There are no specks of despair
we consider small,
we treasure it all—every tiny crevice and every deep well.

We welcome the fearful ones.
We laugh and say,
The crocodiles are only in your head,
you are safe to open your woes to us.

We warmly invite you to sit with your open wounds,
to cry, pound your chest,
express your dejection and confess: *I am so sad.*

We wish for it all to move through you,
and you can travel again,
away from our thick swamp,
whenever you're ready.

We are always right here, already drooping our heads
in honor of your great loss,
in honor of you.

Beautiful Shame Series, Song of the Wild Hearted Woman

I am trapped.
living inside my life's Great Shame Maze,
freezing in my tracks.

Luckily,
the electric fences which make the maze
dictate both my imprisonment

&

my freedom.

The electric fence blares out a familiar refrain:
Don't bring shame to the family.
There is no "off" switch;
you can electrocute yourself
with each wrong thought.

I want out.

I hear whispers of the goddess in me,
loud and clear: *Be free, be free, be free,*
from a wondrous place that feels beyond me.

The electric fence is persistent,
always fully charged.
Each decision is a grueling, disgusting choice,

keeping me glued in place:
Do I please myself and murder the structures that hold me together,
or do I please my kin and murder my dreams?

I want out.

I am terrified
of losing my family's
love and its familiar pull.

Still, the goddess keeps serenading me—
Let's go, let's go, let's go.

My electric fence shrieks back definitively,
No, no, no. Let's obey, let's obey, let's
not lose our way.

I let the goddess's loving calls
drop
like
weak
leaves
to be raked away
into yesterday's mud.

I want out.

Tired of climbing out of conflict

like I'm in someone else's hero's journey,
carrying my survivor's flag to every
so-called-victory.

I must sink into this tension,
stare deeply into
my own shame's eyes,
make contact with my extreme edge,
turn up the voltage,
let the electricity run in me, and
sting and sting and sting.

I can only ascend
by reaching down into the
ditch of painful discomfort.

I make contact with the persecution
of the fence,
so it can lose its hold.

I slow my breathing,
I prepare carefully,
to receive the moving charge

I lean into the line further still, letting it burn
calling myself a *loser, worthless*,
my face is soon a glowing red space heater,
releasing my pain out into the air
that surrounds me,

instead of letting the fences run
hot inside my veins.

And then it happens:
the electric fences start losing their power.
When they begin to turn off,

I turn on.

I suddenly see sparks of my value.

Electric fences are both my confinement

&

my gate into the goddess.

I begin to see there is more than one way
to be good,

I inhale more oxygen,
extend my wings
and lift an inch higher.
Each time, I go higher still.

I am the wild hearted woman
of my dreams.

Beautiful Shame Series, Song of Dreams

This electric fence shook me,
took me out,
on any ordinary day.

It speaks,
You cannot follow your dreams
when you mother could not.

I tell my mom the truth
through my sacred throat,
the flight path between my head
and my heart:

I feel guilty I am following my dreams,
I feel guilty I am making a life that
I want

when you could not.

Speaking the truth out loud—
straight to my mother,
leaning into my perimeter,
the place where I was hurting and hurting,
was my only passageway

into my own power, my own resources,
my whole engine.

Beautiful Shame Series, Song of Desire

This electric fence had a jolt
that bolted me down before I
knew I had a thing called

desire.

The fence speaks: *If you experience your sexuality*
for anything more than your designated groom far out in
your destiny,
then you are smeared
guilty,
a complete whore.

The gouge of the fence is new,
because I only ever doubled down,
ashamed that I was so ashamed,
when others were so freely enjoying sensuality.
Left the whole thing
unspeakable,
pretending to be
just fine,

The whole time, I held
my legs too tightly, spewing hate on my sensuality.
Nobody could tell because
I always imprinted the correct
shapes into the bed sheets.

Bottled-up shame pressed my hands down,

grasping too tightly onto sexuality's zip lines.
Nobody could tell because
I always flew straight across the treetops.

I looked like a laughing bird, comfortable flying in the wide sky,
while my fingers were scraping down on metal wire,
making sure I paid myself in misery.
Held my breath, pretended to soar.

My pleasures were half joy, half doom—
a chocolate-covered rat.

Half release, screaming, *Yes please more.*
The other half contracts,
electric fences prosecute me firmly:
Gross, guilty as hell. You are so bad.
This time, I walk into it, let the fence take me,
letting it singe me with a current or two:
I am ashamed that I enjoy sex.
I am ashamed that my body
can even have it.
I do not feel guilty. I feel I am
guilty. I know I. Am. Guilty.

The empty space around me is sturdy,
carrying the hot and heavy weight of shame so well,
like a good friend, helping me move
my dingiest boxes.

I share my shame across a table of trust.
There is an alchemy in the coffee
when I chat it out, lets me see how
shame and desire are next door neighbors,
sharing the same wall, painted different colors.

My heart begins to question:
Was I good all along?
Is there a such thing as good?
How can this body be criminal for being a body?
Can I live in enrapture?

I am allowed.
I am allowed.
I am allowed to want.

Fresh Monsoon

Wet mud and cow manure splatters
on my hips, my chest.
Mosquitos throng into my home,
teeming with sinister threats,
buzzzzing in my ear,
giving me more things to swat,
hopefully kill.
But I don't;
I never kill
anything.

Even in my imagination,
my rage comes
with built-in extinguishers:
Don't be an angry person. Don't hurt anyone.
I never release the murder fantasy
that could possibly free me.

I block my monsoon anger
so she changes her aim,
blasting forever inward straight through my front door,
slinging her foul-smelling sludge.

I am drenched, practically drowned,
too overrun to swat at any mosquito.

The storm buries me in the couch,
as if I'd worked 16 hours
when all I did was manage to get my head off my pillow

without anyone knowing how hard that was.

I collect more pungent wet soil in every pocket of my body,
and surrender in the worst direction, resigned:
Let the bugs do their worst,
who cares.
My mosquitos feast and feast in my organs for days,
decades.

I am an inside-out umbrella
accepting its delirious storm-ridden shape.

Then one random Tuesday,
I inhale the smell of the muck,
and a fresh monsoon breaks
from inside of me, bursting through
the window of my throat,
and onto an unsuspecting sofa pillow:
I WANT TO MURDER YOU! I WILL
KILL YOU!
I HATE YOU, GOD!

After this deadly outpour
from my mind's fierce creativity,
my target is *completely safe,*
I've murdered *nobody.*
Though I count one more body
in my rage story,
dead.

I vibrate with a new sanity,
a heightened love,
and my view is clarified like ghee.
I see my milk solid facts separate from
the good fat of my anger.
I feel myself climbing out
from inside my skin.

They say anger is reckless, but it is so vulnerable,
it needs cushiony safety to be released wholeheartedly.

Safe in knowing I have never raised my fists this way,
never killed in my entire life.
This fantasy is medicine made from my imagination,
it is my healing, not my undoing.
Safe in knowing my nightmare of a daydream is welcome
in its full bloodthirsty capacity,
in its raw need
to kill.

I keep my exceedingly safe, exceedingly lethal operation
running strong,
tightening my fists in the middle of any day,
to emit my storm in parts,
letting it have its say.

I am no longer eaten alive.
My blood will not be sucked
by the swarms.

I am not my rainstorm,
I am not my umbrella either.
If I am anything, I am a pure verb—
regenerate.

Volcano

A volcano
never apologizes for what she destroys.
Her impulse makes space for her voice.

You are built to unearth yourself,
break through heavy layers of terrain,
expose your truth,

erupt if you need to.

A Billion Years

I used to think anger was so unpretty.
Now I see Luray Caverns
in her unforgiving maddening beauty.

She is built from giving her middle finger
a million times—from above, from below,
from every angle.

She says it so well, so luxuriously, so clearly:
"*Fuck you, I'm beautiful.*"

She is prideful of her shiny empire,
built in any form she pleases.
Her age is her prowess and her glory.

Surrender — make a cavern full
of your honorable anger,
make it your illustrious estate.

You're a billion years in the making.
So yes, you've got something to say.

On Sunny Days, Pigs are Brought to Roast
Previously published by Bourgeon/Day Eight

You came to me costumed in kindness.
You begged for an apple,
I gave you my orchard.
Then you called me stupid
for being so foolish.

You made me your heart's
perverted, pathetic
punching bag.

I walked away carrying a bulk of hate so heavy
I hurt my own back,
flinging it at every other guy.

I hate you from every part of my body—
from my ankles,
my knees, my throat.
I hate you from the feet
of all my ancestors,
and from my heartbeat,
from when I was an ocean fish 400 million years ago.

I was haunted.
Flinching from your ghost attacks.
Exhausted.
I wrung out the sweat
from all my clothes I let myself suffer in

since your last emotional blow years ago.

You left me laying unguarded in an open field
where you lost your personal battles.
Now I remain victorious in my knowledge
I didn't do anything wrong.
It was never me.

I am a wild phoenix who needs to burn it down
to sing her rising song.

You remain sitting there,
slinging back drinks at that outdoor bar,
where on sunny days, pigs
are brought to roast.

May we each muster something of worth
from our soot, from our dust.

Song of Power

V. I. C. T. I. M.

V, I, C, T . . .

. . . . I AM . . . .

. . . NOT a victim.

You took my first time
without my permission,

you took my safety
without my permission,

you took my body's agency
without my permission.

There is one thing I have
that you cannot take from me.
You cannot take my power.

You cannot taste my power.
You cannot touch my power,
because my power rests inside of me,

in the soles of my dancing feet,
in the feet of my dancing soul.

So you can take my first time,

you can take my safety,
you can even take my body's agency.
I will always have this endless
supply of energy
inside of me.

I am my own first time.
I am my own safety.
I am my own body's agency.

I don't have to hide my body anymore.
I am my natural source of light,
shining bright.
a force of my own nature.

It was never my fault.

V. I. C. T. . . .
. . . .O. R.Y.

Why I Spoke Up

I am buckling in on an airplane
when I decide I would speak up.
The engine in my heart is
louder than the roar of the jet.

"I am worth more than this"
is a thought bubble
that floats up, storing itself
safely in the overhead bin,
so that I could collect my thoughts later.

The smell of "Was it my fault?"
lingers, yet to be answered.

They ask that we fasten our seatbelts,
but nobody can secure their gender entirely safe.
Phones turn off, still I hear my message clearly:

Being a woman is workplace hazard.

These loud unspoken words jolt me as the plane lifts off.
Mid-air, I am weighed down
by injustice.
Why should I bear a workplace
that feels dangerous?
Why should I be the one
who flees?

This airplane ride is steady,
thankfully. Leaves me wondering about
the smoothness of the flight my mother took me on,
arriving to this country when I was a little baby.

When the plane lands, I am grounded
in my decision, free to claim my sound thoughts.
In the terminal, passengers scatter into our
co-created society.
I pause to make the call,
I have something to report.

I speak up for my safety,
to restore my full breath,
honor my innocence,
and return the shame officially
to its rightful owner.

On the Other Side of God

I was found out.
It was just a matter of time.

A temple attendant pulled me out
of line with a finality. He must have known—no. He
probably definitely had information on
what criminality lay between my legs.

So when the temple attendant
checked my ticket and papers, and
offered me my spot in line again,
it was too late.
It was too late long ago.

I'd already locked myself up,
called myself a fucking whore.
I'd already inhaled a fog, dark and wintery.
Living on the other side
of god,

My essence vanished.
I moved into a heavy ship, anchored down
by a desperation to be good,
a ship I named
Penance.

Never to set sail to new sights,
to anywhere that might feel good,
feel right.

Therapy's Offer

Therapy's Offer Accepted

I have accepted the therapist's offer—
her drink of candlelight
through the bars
of my sad prison.

I see the impossible glitter of hope
in the blue of my sadness,

just by looking at it
together.

It remains dark, however,
if I don't let her melting wax
do its work,

to look and to notice
what colors appear today.

That power is in me,
to make space,
to sip the light.

Any work we do,
all the effects, small and big,
good and bad,
shall always be what we make together.

Therapy's Offer Bound

It's Sunday night,
and before I crash
into my purple slumber,
I feel the word "we" for the first time.

As if you were the left page,
of the beautiful October *New Yorker*
magazine we both love,
and I the right.

Bound together just fine,
but perhaps the same spine
of a too-familiar story—
that one when I grow so fiercely close.
I am linked so inseparably, I lose sight
of where I end,
and where you begin.

We exist, for now,
along a sturdy-enough seam.
Page after page,
story after story I tell,
we color in all the pictures
together.

Therapy's Offer Confused

I wouldn't just chill,
I couldn't detach.

Afraid
to take my foot off the gas
of my art, or my anxiety,
all the work I was doing in therapy.

Digging and digging
for new things to fix
and fix and fix and fix and fix and f…

But therapy is not an auto body shop.
My life is an in-body experience.

Just because you're a doctor,
doesn't mean I need fixing.
But wait…

does that mean we'd no longer
be driving together
                    at all?

I'm frenzied, I keep
my engine running and running—
with anger for you, with sadness for you, with any intensity
I can invoke to keep the bridge between us nice and strong,

for the chance to keep you with me.
I have to be in-need
to need you,
correct?

If I stop, then I'm left with just one frightening thought:

Where the fuck did you go?

But what if we drove in
separate
cars?

Maybe I could even zoom past you,
and wave out of my window with a smile.

Would the connection of your wave back to me
be enough? Could the airways possibly hold us
together?

It could be that I could stop,
just to say "*Hello*,"
to look at what's alive that day,
and to see how I can need you
when I am fine and thriving.

We practice slowing down the engine.
Sharing one observation at a time.

For now, I drive on my jolting road,
where I run out of gas,
where you are not in my windshield,
where I have to pull myself off to the shoulder to cry,

I make a goal for down the road, or right now:
In between our times together,
I chill in a sky-blue garage that I name
Trust,
the place where I always wanted to go,
the space where I can just
be.

Therapy's Offer Untangling

I blew up, poured my anger's mud on your face,
did all the impolite things
I swore I could never do.

My anger was breathing its fire, alive and fierce right
in front of you.

I confessed my murderous rage—how many bodies
I stacked,
including yours, your children were on my list too,
jealous you might care for them, instead of me.
My childhood's ingredients still raw,
generating fresh material in today's rich story with you.

I used your candlelight of kindness
to set fire to my prison bars.
You remained with me, observing,
honoring the smoke rising from my newfound chimney.

I take vitals:
You did not die,
you did not disappear.
Damage was done.
I'm not sorry for my anger's truth.
And
you're.still.here.with.me.

Gratitude enters the room, warming every corner.
I was not too much for you.
thankyou.thankyou.thankyou.thankyou.thankyou.

Four Showers a Day

Part 1 Punish

Four showers a day
to work to get it all off.
I was shitted on,
felt disgusting every part of the day.

I stained everything in my presence,
I was deep in repentance.

My skin pronounced its judgement —
I am so gross, so gross, so gross.

Some say I was soothing myself with warm showers.
But I was fraught with tension I could not wash off.
punishing myself,
pouring poisonous guilt into my fingers,
working hard to scrub
my shame from my over-showered dry skin,
and clear my name.

But there was never enough soap.

Assault is not in the action, it is in the grime,
the collecting mold,
and the broken tiles

of the long, long aftermath.

Part 2 Witness

I wish to live inside the windows
of my soul,
where I can look in without being inside.
Witness myself.

A new part of me curiously looks through
the foggy shower door at myself,
a blurry silhouette I recognize
so well.

In this new awakening,
I watch myself as I yell and yell,
unclogging my hate through my throat.

From this new position,
I observe my own pressure,
decide to remodel this punishing shower.

Install clear doors that open so easily,
I can walk freely at my own pace.

In my new shower's solid rectangular shelter,
crisp white subway tiles tell me they are in my corner,
allow me to experience my burning heat,
instead of punishing me for my shame, my guilt, and my
rage.

They advise me to never scrub off my mucky feelings
with the harsh exfoliation of my judgment.
They invite me to chant:
I have shame. I have shame. I have shame.
The water is suddenly made warm,
the truth of it softens my muscles.
My shame loosens its grip,
almost vaporizes.

I step out of the shower to moisturize my soul
with a silky vitamin E oil, a bottle of my own compassion,
understanding I am a person who has feelings,
but I am not my feelings—
I am not my shimmering piercing shame.
I am not my gorgeous sticky guilt.
I am not my radiant deadly rage.

I am only my own witness.

Part 3 Bystander in his Story

I find a seat at a park bench next to wildflowers,
who, like me, spend their day asking
whether they are weed or bloom.

The flowers urge me to speak out loud,
to tell the tale of my hundred showers to someone,

a kind confidant,
to say out loud how his saliva had spread his guilt
all over me.

I add to my story: "*I feel ashamed.*"
My companion makes space for my shame to sit on our
bench:
"*Yes, yes, I understand. Shame can be so heavy.*"

I tell the tale of my rage, how I murdered him mercilessly
in my mind,
without hurting a soul.
My friend welcomes it to sit too: "*Yes, yes, rage is so real,*
so ruthless."

Together, we slaughter the weight of the shame by
exposing it,
and a second movie begins to play:

I see how he is the main character of his own history.
I was a bystander,
a background role in his big feature;
just a tree in the way of his major-storm story.

Bright wildflowers continue with their good questions:
Am I sinner, or am I a saint?
Am I a weed that's dirty, or am I worthy?
Am I bad or good?

I make a full colorful crown of them,
celebrating my agency.

I answer my own questions now.

Wildflowers

I held myself tight, safe.
But a dry rose, compressed,
crumbles
to pieces by the weight
of my own glance,
looking at my own terror.
Did those flowers have a chance,
wrapped up so neatly,
taking on the hard work
to avoid being harmed?

I held inside me a scream the size of the Grand Canyon,
so loud it could bring the moon
to its knees.

But my body deserves pleasure,
not a bowl of sugary denial,
that tastes like too much ice cream,
heavy comfort weighs me down,
instead of lifting me up.

And **my Pleasure deserves my alive body.**
I cannot hide from her.
She is a seductress, calls me to surrender,
a siren enchanting me from every corner of my nature.

I spend my oxygen to confess
to an honored soul,
He hurt me. More than I want to admit.

I am not the same person I was before this.

I deserve to take hold of my unrest,
notice it, speak it, give it room
to breathe.

After all, I was never a dried up rose.
I am a garden where wildflowers
were always meant to grow.

Emotional Recovery

When you take a look
under the hood
of your soul,
staying greased up
in your shame,

Don't be surprised if your body
needs to be refilled,
oiled afterwards.

You may be thirsty, hungry,
needing a good wiggle, a good swim,
a good caress, a good inhale,
a good doughnut, a good run,
a good hammock
nap,

before you can rev your engine again and
get to where it is you are going.

Timber! How to Burn Down a Career

It's not the date you say your goodbye, or punch the clock
for the last time,
nor is it the ritual of sending back the computer.

Once you light that match
ending your career,
the flame will feed itself,
heeding its ferocious hunger.

It will take down the entire canopy
of your identity, of WHAT you were,
leaving you with a more treacherous question,
WHO are you?

It will feast happily
upon your original grand master plan,
the gold foundation of your life.

Even when you are nine months
into your new chapter,
you may suddenly need to scatter yourself
and sit somewhere fresh, giving way
to let a giant sequoia tree in your landscape
take its fall.

Let the sadness slowly decompose
to the root of where the idea of your first path
first germinated.

Let the crackle of the fire sound like the words
This is exactly how it's supposed to feel,
drowning out the unhelpful noise of
Don't be sad; isn't this what you wanted?

Let the maddening heat of your grief hit your skin,
and slow you down, until your head tilts down so far,
it feels like
your
neck
fell
off.

Give your sadness time to pay homage
to your past.

TIMBER!
I'll yell it with you

until what used to be
starts becoming a rich
fertile ground.

Graveyard of Friendships

Our friendship ended
without gesture
or closure.
Some days, I trip on the
unburied bones that stick
out in my path.
Have I let you go?
Or do I need to sit in the graveyard
to tend to this wound?

The candlelight of our connection has
dimmed, and
no matter how much ghee
I add to the flame,
it is not rekindling.
It is not one that will light up the whole world,
like I always thought it would.

It's surreal
to think that I might make it into
your airwaves—
peppering a random conversation
with some weird story like
I knew someone once
who always made friends on the metro—
that we could be
ghosts
in each other's stories.

What did I do wrong?
spooks me until I grieve,
scream and scream until I destroy
that distinct room we constructed
in the shape of your face and mine—
that space I would climb into
to see the world so divinely.

Maybe I was borrowing you
and your view the whole time?
Maybe I made up a fantasy of
soul-connected friendship?

Was there anything I could have done?
Maybe? Not?
But maybe
I could have been more assertive?
Maybe?
Anything?
I have different answers, depending on the day.

Some days, the memory is warm but drizzly,
and I stroll in my graveyard
of friendships with happiness, announcing my thank yous
for the impressions made and
the lessons gained.

Other times, my memory is bright and sunny,
it surprises me—

I jog right past,
taking no note of any tombstones,
breathing in the green of the grass.

And there are stormy days,
when I bring a bouquet of white roses,
and a chair for my mucky sadness,
or a tent.
I watch a movie trailer of the friendship,
to grieve, maybe rage,
and emerge, drying off a tear, or a heavy stream
of devastation,
slogging once again towards solid ground.

Pardon me, you're stepping on my Shame.

When the kindergarten kids asked me to bring
bows-and-arrows for
show-and-tell,
they were showing me and telling me I'm different.
I suddenly wanted to play a new game called
hide-and-go-mute.

When the tamarind chutney spilled in eighth grade,
my craving for the tangy-taste was muddled
with pungent shame leaking out of the bottle,
seeping into the carpeting
of my middle school years.

When my grandfather showed up in his turban,
at the bus stop—
the fabric twisted expertly on top of his head-
my warm flurry of love and recognition
was crippled, slightly strangled
by yards of embarrassment.

When my strong lioness of a mother
is misunderstood, has to repeat
her accented English,
my hefty family pride is usurped
by my slimy embarrassment
snaking around the establishment.

Guilt says it would be so treacherous
to be so thankless

for my heritage;

so I bought too many belts, earrings,
denim dresses, scrunchy socks,
cool logo shirts that said "Dance" in neon letters;
but when I saw it, the shirt read "American."

New hats, no Indian wraps.
Scouring rack after rack.
Feverishly checking tags for the right size,
the size of fitting in.
Hoping the clothes could consume my Indianness
from under me, light it on fire maybe.

Covering my shame up with the armor of
teenage garments is like sitting
at a dressing table teeming
with cockroaches,
only commenting on the pretty
perfume bottles.

I take my costuming off my hangers,
turn my ensembles inside-out,
to look underneath.

I inhale the stench
of guilt, the shame of my shame.
Did I hurt my family with my embarrassment?
Can these thoughts desecrate an entire culture?

The double shame always says *yes.*
Guilty as charged.

Thank goodness
the yards of turban embarrassment,
and **the soaking chutney shame,**
did not swallow my family,
never even diminished us.

I am free to feel my discomfort.

When I hear *Don't feel like that, I love*
Indian culture—the movies, the food,
the clothes…

I'll say:
Pardon me, you're stepping on my shame.
I need space to carefully wring out
the muck from my clothes into a bucket,
light up a floating candle on top of it.

On the light days, my shame melts
into grief, dissolves
into a superpower,
a transcendent cultural shapeshifter.

On hard days, I need time
with my bucket of shame
to honor it,

witness it,
sit with it,

letting it exist,
letting myself
exist.

Tinted

I am green,
like the skin of an unripe mango
awaiting her season.
I am green like a neon frog forever lifted,
ready to leap.
I am green like dark seaweed, grieving for her lost roots,
grieving in layers too—the sadness of just how sad it
once was.

I pick green because on certain days,
I want to pour down all my brown
makeup, that gunk into the sink,
for the spectacle of a cleansing,
swirling and swirling until finally
I only see the shiny white
of a porcelain sink—unmarred.
Unmarried, they say I'll stay, if I am too brown.
If I were white, I'd be a clear morning,
I could seize the day.

The lady at Sephora says I have green
undertones—I am relieved.
Green like that mango, that frog, and the
gorgeous seaweed—
the palette of feeling all of life,
In my green camo—I am naked, I am free.
I can seize the whole week, a whole
lifetime—

Still, I am Brown—the color of all the colors mixed into the earth,
into the blanket floor of every lush rainforest.
I am **brown, carrying the fire of my soul inside my skin.**
I am not stained brown.
I am a stained-glass window.
I am not tainted—I am
tinted.

Being Brown in a White Therapist's Office

I am brown.
You, my therapist, are white.

Receiving therapy
is a pineapple green smoothie,
tastes like a summer beach day,
but also leaves the bitter taste of spinach
on my tongue.

Thank you for the natural organic
support and fresh squeezed information.
Still, I hate having to taste it from a group
who deems me invisible,
pushing me inadvertently out
of the majority in the first place.

I wish you could sit on my side of the ocean,
so you can feel how the ice chips fall over here.

The simple presence of your white skin
pushes me into the corner of your office,
I am cramped, having given you more oxygen
before you speak a word.
Years and years of autopiloting
the hiding of my Indianness
makes extra room for you, your skin,
your say on all matters,
even about me.

Makes me cold, makes me want to throw you
into the sharp blades of our smoothie blender.
The history in my body puts you
in heightened authority.
I sit down in my chair
with anger in the air.
Pissed to be pressed down by the weight of
honeydew melon colonialism,
heavy, but hollow and watery.

I resent having to build the cup
into which our work is poured.
Constructing it from explanation after explanation,
just so it can hold. But it never does, it's leaky.
My words are not a bridge; I am not a studied sociologist.
It's not fair.
The juice always spills on my own lap,
trying to codify what it's like to carefully enter
and exit a different castle in the sand,
depending on who is in the room,
or to know how it is to be unintentionally harmed
all day long.

Therapy feels like both a savored hug and an untimely tug
of war against myself,
afraid of breaking down completely.
I am double headed,
both myself and my own mutated ambassador,
assigned the job of making sure you

don't think all Indian people are shitholes
from a shithole country.

Is that my own shame
speaking so loudly in my head, projecting onto you?
Why should I tell you?
I don't like mentioning the bitter
in the stuff we make together,
so you won't think I'm acting like a victim,
ungrateful.

It makes me double down, work extra hard
just to stay in the room,
substituting my family upbringing
to understand the ingredients you use.

But what if I drop the polite toppings,
complained about the smoothie?

What if I brought it back to you,
let it spill, dirtying your furniture,
even vomit some of it,
so we can see it together,
saying out loud: *Hey, can we look at the harsh*
things in our blend?

Can you sit with me, while I share
how it actually tastes? Can I show you
the spinach on my teeth?

I don't want to harbor this heaviness
alone anymore.

We can't unscoop our ingredients,
we only notice them and name them,
understanding
no smoothie is perfect,
ascertaining
if the raw fruit's sweetness
is worth the weight of the green aggrievances.

Conversation after conversation,
stain after stain,
we expand, and expand, and expand
the perimeter
of what our cups
might hold
together.

Beautiful Onyx Shadow

Part 1: Enter

On an ordinary Wednesday at the shopping mall,
my rebel forces send reinforcement.

I wander from kitchen cookware
into the enemy ammunition in the skin care aisle.
Hook after hook, on a long merciless wall,
bottle after belligerent bottle,
cream after caustic cream,
promising to whitewash my joy.

Earlier that day, my mutiny shot its warning fire,
occupying my mind and my hands,
trashing my fresh bottle of acidic skin whitener.

Each bottle on this store's wall reminds me of
childhood warnings:
Stay out of the sun so you don't get dark.
I am in a fight with the sun,
but my arm can't punch the sky,
so I wound myself with words,
proclaiming a declaration of all that is wrong,

Now these products scream my own thoughts.

I want to protest,
sit down on the store tiles
on this extraordinary Wednesday,

and **emit a beautiful onyx shadow**
into the air surrounding me with my dark charcoal thoughts:
You're dark, you'll never get everything you want.
You're dark, you are second.
You're dark, winning is not a thing.

My rebel forces stand steady with their growling voices:
I am tired of hating my own face,
of my desire to exfoliate the color off my skin,
tired of feeling so stupid because my shading is not right.

Still, I wear makeup the wrong color, living as a ghost of myself,
pretending and pretending.

Pert 2: Exit
If you sit with me, I beg you
please
please
please
let me grieve,
let me tell you how I'm so ugly.

If you are blinded by what you cannot see,
If you cannot handle how I feel about myself,
If you cancel my feelings by saying, *But you're so pretty,*

then I'm made even worse, doubling down—ugly plus empty,
devoid of a good brain, I cannot catch up to where you are sitting,
lacking eyes that see what you are noticing.
It makes me put on more white makeup, pretending and pretending
I get what it is you are saying.

I beg you. Please let me grieve, let me tell you
how I am so ugly,
so I can feel through these soggy feelings,
and my foggy glasses can possibly clear up.

The madness comes from sweet, kind people
putting makeup on my self-hate,
bringing bottles of compliments to make up
for my shame, to cover up
my self-loathing, to conceal
my pain.

I wish you could know how disgusting I feel,
how much I want to wipe it off, all my color,
how I can't see my own wedding imprinted into the world,
every union fated as a miscarriage.

Today my grief catches fire,

my chest wants to scream:
FUCK YOU, Lauren. Fuck you and your white, white skin.
You get to have EVERYTHING you want in the world.
Fuck god for giving me this dark noxious skin.

Suddenly I exhale
a tiny moment of relief,
by your witnessing me in my ugly momentary truth.
Thank you, thank you, thank you
for bearing the weight of this.

I bet they can hear my exhale all the way in the
suitcase aisle.
I travel one step into a new place inside of me.
Another exhale, I move slightly further still.
On the other side of that rage and lonely grief, I smile for
my own honey-hued shimmer, at last.
My hand touches my face,
makes contact with my glistening skin,
as if for the first time.

My eyes are clearing up. I may never see exactly what
you see.
Still, I inhale more and more of my natural beauty.
I am delicious in color,
hot masala chai with caramel pecan pie.

I notice more space around me in the wide aisle of our friendship
for both your bright beauty
and mine.

At the shopping mall,
on any given Wednesday,
bring a warm blanket.
The floor is too cold
when I sit alone.
Love is a two-person job.

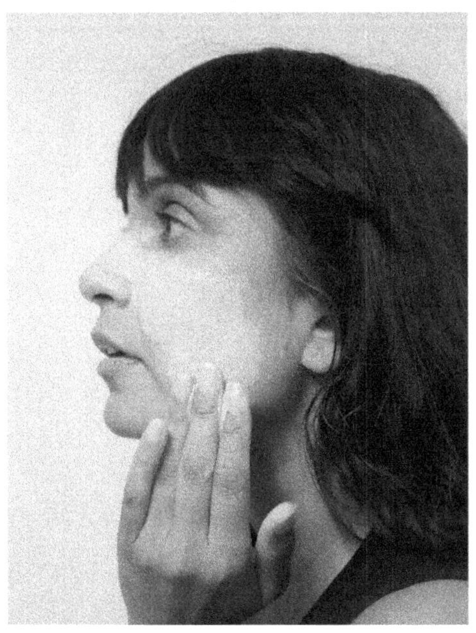

Photo Credit: Ashley Hammond

Blue

What a tragedy it would be
if you let your throat carry
all the weight
of your sadness.
Never even notice it,
never say,
Hi, throat. I see you are too heavy
like a dripping wet towel, needing to be wrung out,
or the soil of an overwatered plant, in need of time.

Don't sit on the lounge chairs of sadness's pool,
pretending to take in the sun
when you want to fold your neck down.

Come put your feet in,
share the treasure of information your
tears wish to speak.
I've already skimmed away the leaves that say,
You shouldn't feel that way,
deep-cleaned the pool floor, taking out the dust of *don't*
be sad.
Wade and wallow for a spell,
melt your own heart.
A wide open pool awaits,
only to sit with your sorrow,

It won't drown me or you
if you share wave upon wave of sadness,

letting an infinity pool fill up
with your brilliant blue stardust.

Red

What a tragedy it would be
if you never encountered
your nurturing force of
anger.

Never breaking a plate
without knowing,
caring about the reason.

Letting your
red hot
murderous rage
swell and surge through your body,
bursting it into a steamy shower.

I even speak it out loud,
from inside this fogged up portal,
made in my wide imagination.

I sink a body to the bottom of the sea,
drowning out a voice
for verbally assaulting me,

cut off an extremity, annihilating their potency
for taking something away from me,

conjure a machine gun revenge, a total obliteration
for violating me so extremely.

Scream so **my lungs eject**
from the chamber of my chest,
directly into my arms,
grateful to be heard.

My anger is an extreme vulnerability,
to be so in touch with life's powerlessness.

Nobody gets hurt
in this imaginary explosion.
A desire to murder does not
a murderer make.
Anger is a revolt made of pure love.

It may feel it will last forever,
but the fireworks eventually
run out of blast, the smoke will clear
to reveal a new truth inside your mind's sky.

I am comfortable with my newfound prowess
to process all this flesh
from a safe and secure
controlled distance,

stacking
bodies,
dripping
blood,
never hurting a soul …

I wondered if I was going crazy,
or already gone.
The whole time, I was going Sane.

I step out from my rage shower,
my mind is cleansed,
eyes cleared.
I see my own place, my own bias
in my injurious story,
emerge an onlooker in this episode
of my serial drama.
I can speak lucidly now, articulating
my needs, making them known.

In the mirror, I am the same
person, not-an-actual-murderer,
wrapped firmly in the soft terry cloth
of my truth,
dripping with sanity.

Heroine's Journey Chapter 7

Urgent yearning to Reconnect with the Goddess

The Heroine recognizes all the feminine energy she has had to strip away, and longs for that initial connection, symbolized by her relationship to her mother

If the poems in Chapter 6 were an exhale, then these poems are a soulful call for replenishment, the desperately needed inhale.

The Stars Conspired

On the day you were born,
the stars **conspired with your ancestors,**
and sent you into the world
with gratitude.

Inhale the Moon and Sky

I handed my power to you,
wore your authority on my body:
your confidence in bed as an anklet,
your influence as a bracelet for my right hand,
your sure-footed walk as a shoe.

You may have taken my breath away,
but you could never claim stakes,
ever.

I won't invent that you are inviting me
into your life
when you take me to your bedpost
or show me your stairwell.

I won't take your manhood
and bottle it up for soap,
or spray it on as perfume.

I take the luxury to

pause.

I can inhale the moon and sky,
exhale stars,
light up my foundation of gravel, brick, cement, mortar.
Heighten my life one stone at a time.

I know a secret that screams to me in orgasmic relief:

I can lift my own weight, exercise my own
authority, deliberately make my own way
into the world.

There is just one last dance step left for us to take.
I will take my own lead, and on the count of three,
when you go right,
I will go
left.

Nectar

They say you run out of time.
But you have to draw it out,
like sap from an impossible tree.

If you harvest your life
from only your logical thoughts,
you miss the nectar.

You have to put your lips to it.

You are here anyway;
you may as well make contact,
taste it, draw it down your throat,

feel its hug in your chest,
let the present moment unearth you.

Shout from Budapest

Inside the dark caves of indecision
inside my palms up hands begging for your permission:
Please just let me live my dream
so my life is made more precious, a jewel on the
Danube River.

In the nickel-a-dozen excuses,
cheap like rain in a monsoon,
in my instant angst, spooned into bland mornings,
behind my languid breath
pushing back the hands of every clock.

There is a wolf
panting and growling,
practically shouting.
Her penetrating presence
sounding off from every corner, every edge, every night.
She doesn't see shadows because she wears them
on her back.
Knows the shape of souls,
isn't afraid of the graves she's made,
dines comfortably in the cemetery
where she buried old friends,
and stacked any number of bodies.

When the detour has gone on for too long,
she grabs time by the throat,
tears it open in cold air,
touches her teeth with her tongue—

The feast has begun.
She eats the sinews of the moment,
drinks in its pulse,
quenches her every thirst.

You may Desire a Slice of Cake

Please stop telling me to look at the sun.
Please stop telling me to smile and say happy upbeat things.
I am more than the pink sweetheart you see in me.
You may desire a slice of cake on a plate
but I am more layered than that.

I will not force myself to face the sun.
Instead I will lean and lean
into my heart,
into my sadness, and my ache,
my rage and relief, my exhaustion too.
I will fall and fall and fall
in love with every
color of me.

When I fall this deeply, I relax
my concrete shoulders and loosen my sticky spine.
I release so far into myself
that the sun will recognize herself
in me.

An Affair with Gravity

Drop
your feet down.
Let gravity have its affair
with your legs, your back,
the nape of your neck.

Do the work to stretch, rise, press, and reach,
but only when you need. For the rest
of the time, let it

fall.

The earth wants nothing more than to hold you up.
Share your weight with her,
rest on her with luxury,

It is the best duet,
the **magnificent choreography** of your life.

She is offering up her resistance.
Dip into its draw,
plunge into its pull.

How else could you possibly
hold up your entire life?

It Could Have Happened Like This

It could have happened like this:

I was never longing-for-love with that lonely feeling
of being forgotten about,

and love was never lost in the woods wandering in the
dark,
heading the wrong way.

Instead, love was always a Sunday morning stroll with
plenty of time.

Every air molecule was already saturated in love, no rush
to make it all add up, no struggle to push through tight
knots I made up in my head.

It could be all I have to do is inhale the love from the
infinite stretch of space all around me.

It could be that just for right now,

I am already where I want to be.

Magic Kaleidoscope Ride

I don't know how to "snap out of it."
Instead, I change the view,
inside out,
by diving into my expanse.

Submerge into your own glorious Red Sea.
Swim inside your green,
kick amidst your blues
through and through,
sink lower in your yellow,
then float straight up
along your gray shadow,
break through the surface—
blink your eyes,
open to the new view.
You are where you're supposed to be,
inside your brilliant color.

Instead of analyzing why you are stuck,
throw on your wetsuit,
jump into your moment of time,
put the sticky kelp of your fears in your eyesight,
then swim around it,
notice every part of it: how does it move,
what does it know, what is making it grow?
Put it in your hands, touch it,
then swim back up and do it again later.

Every time, going deeper still, staying longer and longer,

a mermaid unafraid of her depth,
until you arrive somewhere new,
a more vibrant, colorful view.

Take this magic kaleidoscope ride,
explore the infinite ocean of your heart,
so you can float inside a new pink balloon of time
and space,
where you are carried along and sheltered
by your own warm kindness,
your cool curiosity,
and your powerful presence.

Light of the Whole Sun, a poem about Identity

I step into it again,
that wet mud.
It soaks through my socks
and it feels like Monday morning.

My knuckles turn white from holding onto a flag so tightly,
I sink into the mucky sadness.
The flag was never real anyway. The one, maybe ten I
hold onto—
Female, daughter, artist, worker, American, east coaster,
city person, spontaneous, dancer, wise…
The flags are never true.
They are each just a single hue of my whole prism.

Let the yellow flag in you and the blue one mix into a
mystery green.
And let them all be baffled when your purple fades
into gray.
It's laughable—to think we can sit so still
becoming one identity,
when the entire planet we live upon
constantly moves and moves, expands and expands, and
opens again and again;

Even when you think you're done and say,
Ah, I have landed. I have arrived. I know myself!
Even then, there shall come a moment
when your being feels too small yet again,
craves more oxygen—

like **an incredible creature tapping at its own shell—**
asking to be released, please, once again.

Free yourself from the sludge of forcing yourself
to fit in. Walk comfortably to elevated ground,
where you don't have to sink into the mud too far,
and where you can inhale,

where you can drop your irritation at expectations,
and look to your own hands to see which flags
are clutching to you.

But don't let go,
keep those flags—they are your lovely colors.
Let loose your hold.
See them fly and flip in the wind. They are soaring kites
on a summer day, high above,
where you see the light of the whole sun first,
before you catch sight of a single kite.

Friendship is a Place

Our friendship is a ready river
of vulnerability that gurgles
in the undercurrents with *I love you* and *it's safe here.*
It is a place to jump into, swim,
laugh at the scene we are in,
and share whatever is present for us.

But if I unintentionally splash
water into your eyes,

or if my words are an oil spill
of miscommunication
into our flow,

then may we both reach into the water
and sit with the gunk, tending to it carefully,

you—opening your tributary of the truth, the dark waters
of how my words harm you, making clear how they land,
how they reverberate in you.

Me—receiving the flow of fresh knowledge,
digging into the floor of our friendship,
apologizing, changing my path by cultivating new inlets,
new passageways,
closing up unhelpful ditches,
deepening our capacity—

As evening appears,
we toast as we watch the glorious sunset,
knowing we each contain more than enough
rich mineral for fresh new bonds to take hold.
We are each already
quite whole.

Dare to Share

Invite The Great Shame Monster
to your two-person picnic,
as a timed-entry guest.

When it appears, offer it plenty
of food and water.
Ask: *So, what's your story, Shame Monster?*
What makes you tick?

Let it stick to its simple script,
let it stay on message,
let it sell you all its books and bumper stickers.

Let it **talk itself out loud into disappearance,**
until your picnic basket weighs
about 50 pounds lighter.

Warm Bath of Silence

She punctuates her day often in a warm bath,
not because she is already drenched in exhaustion,
not because her sinister stress spiders into her sleeves.

She simply switches out her mind's frenetic songbook,
playing a new one where the notes stop
more often.

She pauses before the music builds up so much tension
that the bath overflows with her cold frustration. She
comes to a complete stop
before she is defeated, before she is submerged in heavy
sadness, blue without enough oxygen.

She stills herself to immerse
into a **clear water tranquility,**
made from her inaction.

She works to lull herself because her true melody
needs her to take her fingers off the piano keys,
requires her to slow her voice down to a hush, to breathe
more air.

She knows her next honest and crisp note
can only come from her well-oxygenated
silence.

She draws a warm bath of quiet,
and soaks into her being
any time during her day.

Extreme Cleavage

That cool fall night, I could sense my breasts.
I didn't need a significant other;
I felt so significant already.
I stepped with a new dignity,
a firm and formidable regality.

My extreme cleavage suddenly was my location,
never lost, always found.
When I walked, it led me,
and laid out before me a soft white carpet
for my liquid soul.
Everywhere I went, I took with me my milky possibility.

My breasts spoke so crisply that night:
I can provide for myself.
I can provide for others.

Thriver's Guilt

Dear goddess ancestors,

Let's gather by the well,
lift the hefty
sadness of our shared history,
moaning with each new bucket full,
letting our hearts become a chorus
of grief, as the well sings to us:
I'm sorry, I'm sorry, I'm sorry.

Let's gather by the river
to wash our saris on the hard rocks,
beating out mango-shaped sweat from the hard
work that took the place of ripe passions
and fresh dreams.
Our washing bats and scrubbing boards
screaming in unison,
Injustice, injustice, injustice.

Let's squat down at the open fire
kitchen to make a meal,
eyes always blurry from the smoke-stained decision
to put everyone else first.
We will season our food with our own kindness,
feed each other with bare hands,
give thanks for our own efforts,
each morsel repaying its ounce of gratitude:
Thank you. Thank you. Thank you.

Let's rest outside the temple
so we can wash each other's feet,
smile at each other's ankle bracelets,
and ask one another, *What shall I pray for today for you*?
Let's look into each other's eyes,
and let that gaze be a shelter that whispers,
I love you, I love you, I love you.

Before we make our way back,
let's circle around the well once more,
hold each other's shoulders
so our throats can
charge out the sorrow—
our grief about all this grief,
so we don't hold ourselves
in the purgatory of lament.
Let's weep,

until our lungs
are so full of air,

we float.

Let's meet at the rooftop,
to sing one last song to say
goodbye.
Let's dance with whatever
feeling each one of us is in,
as long as we dance together,

in each other's company.
Let's send each other off
back into our beautiful flight paths
with lanterns that chant:
I see you. I see you. I see you.

The wind invites each of us
into her only melody—
I am allowed to be free.
I am allowed to be happy.
I am allowed to be
as I am.

Heroine's Journey Chapter 8

Healing Mother/Daughter Split

In this chapter, our Heroine now expresses her authentic raw devotion to the feminine, and to her own mother whom she first had to reject, to push into the more masculine realities of the world.

My poetry here is about connecting with other women in my friendships. I also include the uncomfortable passageways to experiencing real love and respect for my most important relationship, the one with my beautiful, strong heroine of a mother.

The Taste of Guilt

My mom stands in her position rolling wheat dough
into miraculously tiny little circles.
Older sister stands in her place to her right,
frying them up, laying them down.
I take my seat at the table, counting the seconds of my life,
the tiny pani puris, careful not to crush them.
One, two, three, four…
all the way to 200 in each container.

My mother comes by my station, adding a few extra in
case any break on the way.
Nobody else can make them so sturdy
and yet melt-in-your-mouth like she did.
She took orders and orders and orders,
and desserts too—hundreds of silver-coated
diamond-shaped pieces of her love.

She holds a loud dream in her chest,
fragile like the instant crumbling of a pani puri.
She was always decidedly wife first.
Her dream of a full restaurant business remains raw,
uncooked, untasted.

Here I stand free to savor my dreams.
This freedom is bitter, dusted in guilt,
undigestible,
a made-up meal feeding a lump in my throat,
always making my belly hurt with the piercing question:
Who was I to feast on my dreams

if she was always to be starved of hers?
This acid culpability reaches my organs,
eats me alive.

Suddenly I notice how my guilt is a disguise for anger.
Easier to let the sharp rage puncture me,
than let my wrath kill my own mother.
I don't want her to die.

But anger is a smoky paprika shade of love.
It is made entirely of deep love.

Seething like the hot oil, why can't she see me
for my dreams?
When she combs my hair, why can't she also receive
the strands in my mind that tell her who I am?
Why can't she know all of me?

Burning through my anger's fuel, I arrive at the taste
of grief,
letting go of a mother I made up in my head
so I can be nourished from the bustling enterprise
of her motherly love. I taste her kindness in the soft rotlis,
and her keen eye on my happiness in the glossy ghee
she pours so generously on top.

Now I see a little more clearly:
my mother walks on her own richly flavored path,
as I lay out my own way, a fork in my own road,

rather than a knife that cuts us apart.

We can always sit at the same picnic blanket,
scooping enough onto each of our separate plates,
to feed our own needs, then have a laugh together
for dessert.

Sari to Skin

The edge of an ocean touches earth to form
a boundary,
a place to live, call home.

Still, my body is the landscape inside which I breathe
and roam.
My skin marks my borderline,
the one Indian aunties point to, paint too
much shame upon.
Don't wear short skirts,
Steer clear from deep Vs
Off the shoulder—off limits!
Instructions for my crop top belly shirts:
hand them down to your nieces.

These same women, who at family parties,
wear a single strip
of nine yards of fabric.
The bottom edge stays long, straight, perfect.
but all the rest—the body's valleys and hills
exposed freely.

Midriffs peek
out of petticoats, forming enticing ripples.
Necklines reveal arresting cleavages.
Sari blouses hook on tightly,
Divulging vulnerable ridges on backs, visible to everyone.
Bodies without shame,

captivating
in their comfort.

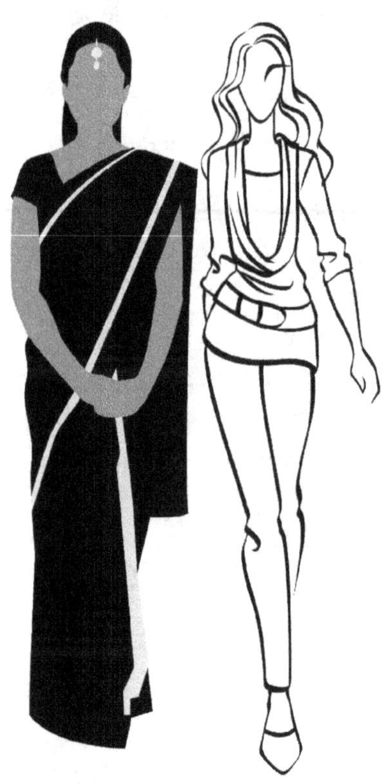

Self Rage is Self-Love

I kept my own Rage against myself
handcuffed,
thinking she was dangerous,
believing she would bring me to my end.

But she was the one with the
key.

When I couldn't hold her in,
I let her heat misdirect to
my mother,
in the too-short sentences I'd spit her way.
But today,

I let rage fly straight to myself,
a capacity I had no idea I retained,
calling myself whore and cunt,
telling myself I am bad and couldn't have any money
or happiness,
banishing myself to loneliness for the rest of my life.

I invited Rage in,
made her a plate and let her be herself and rage,
even fed her raw garlic and onion
so she could flare and flare and flare
up and out at me.

Until she dropped to her knees:

I didn't want to, I didn't want it. I didn't want to have sex that day.

All she wanted was for me to hear
that sound of my own truth.

Until she keeled over:

I'm sorry. I'm sorry. I'm sorry.

I feel my mind tugging on her sari.
It was never my mother I was mad at.
It was always
me.

Until she revealed her depths:

I forgive you. I forgive you. I forgive you.

Rage always had my salve, my milk, my honey
deep inside her full belly.

Finally, I can look
into my own eyes,
and I can look
into my own mother's eyes,
with my full capacity
to love and love and love and love and
love.

Legs

Would you cancel your entire winery
trip if a single serving
would taste too sharp,
needed to be aired out?
It's unthinkable that you'd be compelled
to run home if the glass were
undrinkable
for just a spell.

If we are in bed together,
and suddenly my body changes its clocks,
so it's January of that one year all over again,
when it was too cold to walk,
and instead of being in these silk sheets with you,

I am transported into a yellow cab with that man who
helped himself to my hands, my thighs—

don't jump and run home.

Let's make a game.
I get to say, from anywhere on the bed, *Let's take a break.*
You'll pause,
putting down our burgundy passion
to let it settle
for just a spell.

After we relax,
my clocks get reset

just by chatting into your kind eyes.
I look around the room, ask about
that oversized blue painting again, make fun
of your crazy coat collection on display,
until I am delivered back
to the present time.
Suddenly you look
so drinkable
again.

We start again slow, observing the wine's
legs and how they want to flow, registering
their desires before picking up the glass again,
imagining our next mouthfeel.

I say: *Ready, if you are,*
and you kiss my words.

We name the breaks
"buzz kill" and laugh every time,
but they do the opposite.
They increase the deep cabernet
heat.

It's sexy.
In this long pour of time,
my muscles ease even more than before,
my skin becomes a wide-open vineyard,
open to its juicy possibilities.

Plucked away from my safety dismay,
I am present to your
full body.

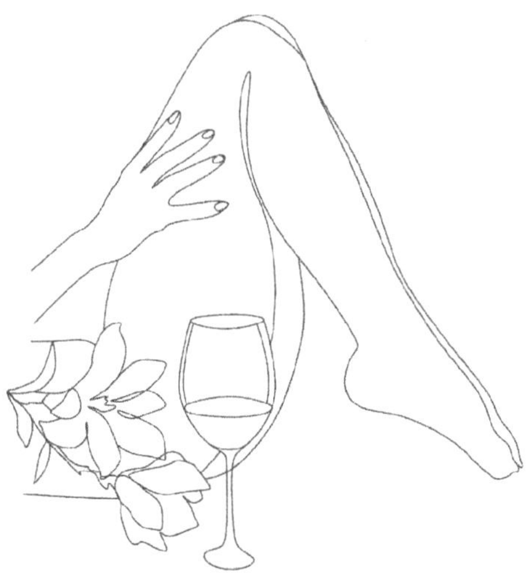

The Birth of Self-Love

She sits tall, pretty too,
but you don't notice
because her goddess prowess proceeds her.
Demeter is the mother of goddesses who travels the
entire earth in search of her daughter,
lost in an underworld.
The mother to all of us,
she cries your tears and flies for you,
waits for you to finally see her, take her soft direction,
and sit inside her impenetrable blossom fortress, warm.
The opposite of a cocoon,
she does not wait for the future.
Her inhale takes in the world
as it is now and brings it back to you softer.

She watches you give the world empty glances.
When your eyes are past their last teardrops,
which are the goddess's first teardrops,
it is her first time to catch you, relish you.

When every woman in your life—
mother, sister, leader, a lifetime's best friend—
heads into her own life,
Demeter
will sit with you as you grieve,
wailing with you for all the losses you must lament.

Demeter writes down your life with great intention
in her richest deepest blue ink.

You are her main protagonist.
She will always live up to you,
offering an indigo love you deserve.

She's taken the train, arrived
early for you,
She always has triple the time.
She'll wait and watch for the rosy ribbons of life
to float back to you.

Demeter listens to what you're not saying
as you contract your existence into
your own personal Hades, the hellish spaces
inside your head.

Go softly with yourself,
wait in your hush to hear her voice,
to receive her wherever her beginning
starts for you,
whenever you let her catch your heavy head
to rest upon her.
Clear out a soft sofa in your heart
for her to breathe in your home with you.

Soon the pages in your book will turn themselves again.
Demeter will place her hand on yours,
enjoying your next word, letting your voice
intwine with hers.

Fall upon the cushion of your own arms.
Let yourself sleep,
may your soul forever see rose gold,
that feeling that you are good,
you have goodness.

Demeter
was always you.

Community is an Inside Job

Community is not a place
you can point to on a map.
It is not a public square,
nor a set of Zoom squares
we can easily stare at.

It is invisible thread
made from our hearts'
sheer
desire to connect.

A thread sourced
from **our soul's raw fleece.**
May we always be in touch
with our own infinite fields.

Let's gather our spinning wheels, and our spools—
all our tools to create more and more intimate lines,
weaving together a beautiful intentional design,
co-created,
made from our intrinsic, remarkable twine.

Rani Vibes

A practice in real royalty—Ranis,
we each sit in our own thrones,
but we cannot fix each other's crowns.
All I can do is shine and shine and shine mine.
So if hers tips over, falls to the ground,
she can catch sight of her light
when she glances towards me.

We South Asian women
don't have to sit in made-up hierarchies.
We arrange ourselves in a circle,
reminding one another of her power.

I love each Rani in my sphere.
She has a depth born into her skin,
carries two or three worlds
in one hand.

Her stunning eyes
shoot a vibrancy so rich,
that wherever she looks,
bright colored clouds
lift into the air,
a shiny Holi celebration
inside her every glance.

She is a powerhouse.
A goddess landed next to me.

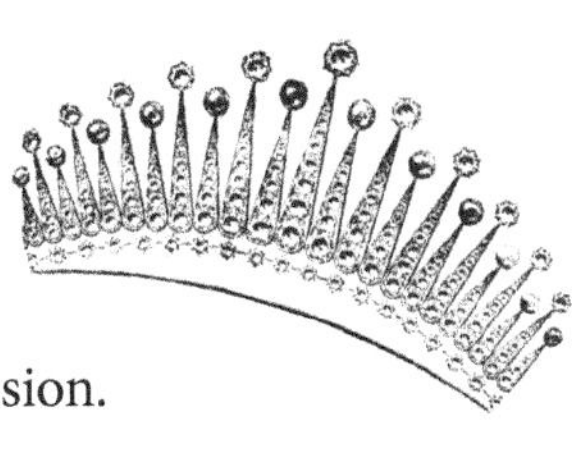

Her kajal lines her vision with precision.
If she aims for her desire, she fires.

Her bangles ring like my mother's,
she sounds
like home.

River of Intuition

I want to swim in that luxurious swelling
River of my Intuition.
You know the one,
you don't have to hike that far to get there.
It's always in front of you instantly.

It dips like the backs of my knees,
it rises and falls like my belly.
It won't be destroyed like prey,
it won't be torn apart like countries,
it can never be separated from nature like an orphan.

This River does not know the difference
between a bad day and a good one.
It accepts all of life so radically,
gushing, and rushing, then slowing
her pace, and jumping again, laughing as she falls,
unintentionally changing the shape of silver stones
on her way, feeding young sprigs with her spray.

I don't graze my hand in the River,
I bow my head, immerse myself,
honored that my body's shape is traced inside her.

She makes room for others—surrendering her space for
hips, elbows, thighs, and toes.
She makes room for mushy green moss,
for every shape of fish,

enough room for every tooth of every alligator,
every tiny pebble thrown in.

This River knows herself,
knows she is already so full,
knows that she knows enough, that she is her own source
of information, sufficient.
She dances to the sound
the planet makes as it spins around.
She collaborates with your tempo too,
absorbs your life easily into her expression.

Don't nurse her.
She is voracious, can feed herself.
Don't turn her into your warm bay
that begs to melt it all away.

She is cool, cold even,
prefers to stir you,
keep you wide awake.
Listen loudly,
her message is never meant to be heard in whisper.

She never stops to pose for photos, or fake a smile.
Her flow is not a notion for you or me to pronounce.
It is her first and only roaring choreography
forever trusting her own pulse,
her impulse to
move wildly.

Diamond in the Collection

Don't tell me I am a diamond
in the rough.

After I witness each of my facets,
my surfaces begin to reflect
light,
they are exquisite
exactly as they are.

I found the diamond
in me.

Now all I see are diamonds
all around.
Helping another jewel woman rise
deepens my clarity,
elevates my quality.

Scintillating circles of women are aggressive
in their love,
a volcanic pressure of pure, fierce belief
is exactly what formed us in the first place.
We recognize the other is rare, worthy,
concentrated in value.

I am not a solitaire stone in her lonely setting.
If a woman dazzles me and the air around her
with the flicker in her eyes,
help her keep her shimmer.

I am a diamond in the collection,

a spectacle of luster and
brilliance.

Divine Infinity

You were born innocent.
Guilt is a disguise for something else—
your anger, your fear, maybe your regret.

You are free to feel
through all your rises and your falls.

Keep riding the infinity sign,
as it **continues and continues,**
carrying all of you,
for as long as you need.

Your giddy excitement
into your enormous fury.
Your wholehearted happiness,
into your deepest misery.

Sip your clean air.
It will not diminish the oxygen supply elsewhere.

Laugh with a full belly.
It will not make someone else's plate empty.

Celebrate a wild accomplishment with a wild party.
The confetti will not suffocate another body.

The divine infinity invites you to hop on board.
Take it for a surf,
you were born innocent,

let it cruise you into those dark places,
let it raise you into the brightness,
keep riding it into your destiny.

Reclaiming her Name, Passing the Mic to my Pussy

Don't say the word pussy in vain.

When I think about my pussy,
I feel so damn rich.

When I look, it's a city where the streets are made
of gold,
and the clothes are laced in jewels.
The wealth of 30,000 worlds is kept
safely under my belt.
It's my own personal house of abundance,
and the world is my playground.

So I will hop, skip
and jump you.
But can you handle it,
if I pounce, and spread
my power around you?

I am switched on when the rain
drenches everything,
because I am the same.
I will rain, I will pour,
I can flood you.

Don't say the word pussy in vain.

She doesn't wait for you
to rouse her.
She will wake you,
take you, make you
ask for her all over again.

Heroine's Journey Chapter 9

Healing the Masculine Wound

Here, our Heroine notices that the masculinity she acquired was not necessarily one that was supportive. It was tainted with a forceful erasure of the feminine. This imbalance leaves the dial turned up too high on the controlling, overly aggressive, even destructive energies.

The poetry here touches on this disparity. Virility is expressed in the form of decisiveness, action, and forward motion, in a way that supports me more holistically.

Power Through

I was a lawnmower,
forcing my ear-splitting engine on,
muffling my desires to be soft,
to connect, to make space.

The machine rattles on,
blowing its persistent song:
Don't be a wuss. Just power through.

I made a pristine well-manicured
career,
perfectly rectangular.

Mowing over my wildness,
cutting up wishes and pleasures,
throwing out extensions of myself
with the grass clippings.

The Melting it was Made for

I stay pissed at my father,
angry he will never really get who I am,
an artist, not engineer.

As a child's first love,
I wished to be so enjoyed by him
that he could gobble me up,
consuming me with all his attention
until he and I were one.
He was my puppeteer; I needed to know
my every step would delight him.
All grown, I look to the ceiling from the floor,
my eyes widen, I'm dead in my tracks, frightened to see
there are no puppet strings,
horrified to know

there is no puppeteer.

Am I abandoned?
Do I exist? How could we be in kinship,
if I move in any which direction
that could be wrong, breaking our unifying connection?
Terrified to be so exposed,
how do I know which way to go?
Following my dreams freezes me.
He believes in me so fiercely, loves me so deeply,
but this need to be seen for who I actually am
uproots me from my very soul.

Living in longing is a constant friction,
falling from the puppet stage,
onto my risky ice rink, forever scraping by.
My blades keep me upright,
and leave me
on the brink
of a great fall.

What if I let myself
c
o
l
l
a
p
s
e
Hit the hard ice, **let my heart crack.**
I grieve that perfect duet with him.

One that will never be, and never was,
leaving me wondering, can there be safety
in my own personal choreography?

Through my nutritious tears,
my view starts to clear—we were never the same person
in the first place,
always functioning on separate operating systems,
deeply familiar strangers.

His eyes beam into life's prism,
to take in his own view.
My eyes do the same,
but they gift me a completely different story.

At once, this distinction is so isolating, so maddening, so
very upsetting—why
can't I give him my eyes, so he can see exactly what I see.

&

it is so life-affirming, so invigorating, so enriching—how
profound to know so many kaleidoscopes can exist at once
without colliding.

My icy surface thaws into solid ground.
My eyes soften with every blink to see my father has his
own 360-degree view.
My puppet strings dissolve into conversations, questions,
and truths.

I make a lifetime
of watching my heart
do the melting it was made for.

Lion

A lion's chest is broad and deep,
not because he is proud of his muscles.

It is grand because it is from this immense
chamber where he fights tooth and nail
to keep his vulnerable heart soft, happy,
alive.

He measures his kingdom
by the capacity inside his chest.

The Wrong Horse

You never put in your
vulnerable stallion.
You choose to send in the counterfeit,
placing only half your wagers on the table
and hanging back, hiding the truer rides
in the shadowy stables.

If you're debating whether the gambling counters are clean,
then they're likely dirty,
regardless of how divinely
your white-trim dress matches your wide-brim hat,
or how much shine is on your patent leather loafers.

You can place a bet at the derby,
but if you put in the wrong horse,
your smiles, your winnings won't feel as shiny
as the photo finish.

Let's wipe the scoreboard and start again,
build a different racetrack.

Where we learn in small steps,
how we are safe to let ourselves trip,
fall, crash.
Let our open wounds air out, one
centimeter at a time, or
all at once if you wish.

The new track is round, whole,
it sits much deeper, you have to
first
drop
in.
No hot gunfire
to claim fictitious beginnings, nor
final flags marking a fantasy finish.

Only empty space to run freely,
and plenty of corner fences to try leaping
wildly,
knowing **everything is always**
just practice anyway.

The stakes are higher in this venture,
you're risking your embarrassment
for the chance of the lottery win
of real connection.
Points for every honest feeling revealed
without explanation,
points for every confession received
without an inner roll of the eyes.

It is not that we are all
winners.

The point
of the honesty game
is to keep on playing.

Love, Lust, Money, and Thirst

I tossed a coin into the water fountain on Diwali
making the usual holiday wish for good fortune.
I wish to repaint this memory now.

As I imagine releasing the copper penny,
I add another wish: *I wish to be free.*

I take my aspirations for a gold fortune, glistening homes,
legendary love stories,
and soften them, make them just one part
of my whole kaleidoscope vision, not the entire focus.

I cannot see the show from my seat, I am too close.
I cannot watch my whole life playing out
if I am the one in it,
hot under stage lights,
blinded, not knowing where I am in the reel of things.

I must step back, take notice if my wishful coin is stained
with "yeah right" or "probably not me,"
or, worse, detained by *I will only be happy when…*

Send in your coins with wishes of love, lust, money,
and when your hand opens to the water,
release your stringy attachment too, all that craving.

The hunger for hunger keeps me
starved.

The desire for desire keeps me
desperate.

Throw away the thirst;
trade it in for all the
Trust.

Letting go

Take my conductor's baton.
I refuse to hold the count for every instrument,
and the beat of every song ever played.

Release me, please, from this fantasy of an
invincible position.

Let me sit, settle my torso another centimeter into the
audience side,
where I don't dictate nature's correct pathway
for her free birds in flight; and delight instead
in their random track,
and their impulse-led flock-trades instead.

I stop maintaining the axis around the earth
to hold my whole big show together.
It was never in my job description
to drop rock-heavy milestones
into earth's passageways.

The teachers advise, *If you choose to control,*
you will fail anyway.
So I let some balls fall to the ground,
not all the through-lines are mine.

Here—take all these controls, the batteries,
and my stop watches.
Take away my weak glue too, so I can stop pressing my life
forcefully into sticky sham stories,

barely staying together.

I surrender. And I

d
r
o
p

into a vast ocean that catches me,
a place where dreams take greater shape,
where orange fish and golden rays breathe deeply,
where coral fluorescence shimmers through its shame,
where bold black whales move without hesitation, glide
in long-distance joy unimaginable.

I am diving in, so I can
give birth to mystery,
and to my laughter.

Permission to say "I Don't Know"

I don't know
makes me stupid
like a broken watch,
or a pen out of ink.
The panic ensues—

Will my checks be cancelled?
Will they take away my house?
I'll be found out,
left behind,
dead from starving of love.

I am suddenly muddled.
How can I look you in the eyes
if behind mine is
insufficiency?
All the things unknown-to-me have teeth to bite me.
My shame spews out made-up answers to protect me.

Until finally I let these shameful thoughts sting open
my heart,
confessing that my lack of information feels the same as
lack of intelligence, capability, worthiness.
But I am not a catalogue
of all the things I know, I am more than that.

I suddenly see each person only knows a speck
of stardust in the universe of everything perceived.

The most vibrant new chapters always begin with
a resounding question,
waiting for its well-nourished answer.

Let's drop our heavy heads on the silky bed
underneath the question,
melt inside quilts hand-stitched in "I don't know"
and fall asleep,
letting the unknown seep in, cozy
in the **luxury of immense wonder.**

The Truth About Courage

The only instrument I need
is a good stethoscope.

I listen to the warm, strong passageways inside.
My bloodstream always knows
which way to go.

I decide I can tune the world
outside of me to match the quiet
inner frequency of my truth.
I call that courage.

Do not call courage combat boots and suffering.
Courage is a softening,
like candles melting
to see their own luster.
Courage is not coerced,
it is released from delicate vulnerability.
Any disruptive commotion that might ensue
is just the aftereffect
of the trusting, **the quiet knowing**
what's already true.

I keep my stethoscope
forever around my neck,
and my ears ever tuned in,
until courage becomes an extension of me,
growing like my wild hair,
inevitably.

Nationhood

I'm too Indian to be American.
I'm too American to be Indian.

In India, where I was born,
I was moved to the foreigner's quarters in an ashram
that smelled, looked, felt just like the temple
in New Jersey where I was young;
pronounced as an American
by my walk.

This body marks me Indian in color,
American in movement.
I was not at peace in the temple bosom
of my motherland.

At home in America I didn't coordinate well with
blonde,
allowed to date,
shoe-wearing-inside-of-the-house
Americans.
It is painful to have one ear that hears
only Indian sounds
and another that picks up only American vibrations.

I've tried being both in different company…
But it gets confusing.
I never know which flag to pick
Neither one fits my mixed-up true self.

That's why I hold citizenship in **a land**
the shape of my two feet.
Where I step
forms the boundaries of a nation
I call *Myself.*

With each move I make,
the bells on my dancing feet
ring to the beat of
my humanity, my hope,
my nationhood.
And it feels like my life just started—
I could dive into my destiny.

Only I know which step I want to take,
which direction I want to face
in comparison to the wind.
Sometimes I want it to carry me.
Sometimes I want to walk against the forces of air.
Sometimes I just want to be with the air
and breathe.

Only I know
The truth of my
citizenship
In this land
where I stand—
red white and
blue

like sapphire
like the meaning of my name
blue diamond
the strongest stone on earth.

My own personal territory
with no categories!
Just light reflecting
inside of me.
America, America, America
I am
home.

Rebel Tendency

Pushed, shoved square pegs
inside a round soul.

But, I am not misshaped,
and don't need reconstruction
or sanding down.
I put away my sawtooth
judgement.

Rebelling is my nature.
I am not trying to be difficult.
I fire on all four cylinders.

I run so that I can catch
the feeling of the air
on my ears.
Someone else can measure my miles.

I will do my dishes
to launch from a sparkly morning.

I can box myself in with impressive right angles
made from the word "should";
but I always climb out from a spiral
path, listening for
the inner vibration of the word "YES!"

My angular to-do lists written on square post-its,
and the sharp gridlines of my calendar
puncture the round bubbles of my vast energy.

I am a rebel,
busy expanding
into my round being.

The Sweat of an Artist

When I work, I spend my soul.
Sinking in, digging out
my insides,
making drafts
upon drafts,
upon drafts,
sifting out the gold from the debris.

Artists are not **gods**.
We make space for the goddess
to deliver what she wants to say.

We are laboring to make contact,
constantly intertwining our thoughts, senses,
and intuitions,
stringing them together with our 13-billion-year universe.

We employ our inhale to take it all in,
recruit our courage to exhale it,
expend our embarrassment to share it.

We invest too in our recovery, kicking back up ever slowly
to full buoyancy,
after the deep exposure from our soul's perilous
cave-diving.

We may be ecstatic to gather deep-sea pearls
and jewels from our conscience for our life's work.
Still, it is not a clean illusion, a cursory trick,
or a quick fusion.

It materializes
from the sweat
of an artist.

I am not my work

A singer's voice
is in the air,
it cannot be the same as her.

A landscaper must
leave the garden behind,
as he walks away.

My work is of me,
it is not me.

My work could easily be
a stranger I greet on the bus,
wearing my same perfume.

You cannot diminish me,
if I give you my stuff.
I cannot be consumed
by what you make of it,
it is not me.

I am free to release my work from me.
I am free to release myself
from it.

The Truth about Celebrating

I receive a bright bouquet
to celebrate
a big win,
my success,
the next chapter.

I let the colorful flowers flounce their fragrance
as I twirl and squeal,

&

I let their **green leaves and stems sit**
with me as I grieve.

Every celebration comes with its custom
wet napkins, spilled champaign,
fallen cakes

When I make something new,
I celebrate a glorious spin in my destiny

&

cry for the collapse of old formations
that once held me up.

Let's serve the cake!
And when we set the table for a good and proper toast,
save a seat

for all my sadness too.

It is only when my sorrow gets to eat,
that my cake can taste so sweet,
drizzled in honey gratitude.

In Your Own Hands, a Poem about Patience

You may scream into the fridge in frustration
and with kind eyes, tell yourself,
be patient.

But maybe patience is not what you are craving?

Perhaps you are asking instead
to put the needle back on the record you stopped,
the upbeat steady song, written just for you.

You turned the whole machine off,
saying, *I'm not going to do anything,*
not even breathe, until I'm successful.

You are the DJ—your joy lives in your own two hands,
When you are asking for patience,
perhaps you are asking your heart
to take a step back, see the dance you are already in.

You blinked your heart shut.
Perhaps you are asking to open it up,

It was always just rehearsal
anyway.

Plug the record player back in,
to listen to your pleasure, your birthright,

You deserve the hug of the present moment

as you are, right now.
The future was never your business.

Fill your own hands
with ample love
to do any task.

Next time you scream into the fridge,
take in the sight of the bright red apples in front of you.
Even a trained expert will miss her shot
if she thinks about anything
other than the juicy moment
already in her own two hands.

Poem from a Boy inside of a Girl

Hi, is it safe to come out?
Hello?
Can anyone hear me?

I'm tired of speaking on this cut-off mic.
I'm tired of staying angry that you keep unplugging all
my wires.

Hello? I want more.
I want more decisions.
I want more transactions.
I want to come out into the world more often,

not just when you need to use me.

I want to make swift decisions,
not caring what the world thinks,
putting my masculinity on full display,
not focusing on the chinks
in my armor.

You hang back too much
waiting for the stars to align.
I already have a strong ladder all the way to the sky,
put me to work.

I'm not someone who has a lot to say.
I'm someone who has a lot to do.
I am your best agent. I am your god—

send.
Stop paying so much attention to how I look.
Give me your time.
Don't worry, I've already written our playbook.

You have shut me out, worried about being found out
that you are a boy, that you are
me.
So you cage me up, and let loose your rage.
The hair on your chin, your breasts, your legs,
your arms, your back, tiny strands that always spelled out
"boy" and "man" to you, and made your young mind
question this:

Would you ever be a woman? (Yes, of course, you
already are.)
Is there a man in you? (Yes, hello, that's me.)

You walked out of the blue-tiled bathroom of your
childhood,
after the mirror told you that you were, in reality,
a boy.
Your own startling thought
became your instant truth,
and your confusion,
and the shame ensued.

Stop trying to kill me—
you can't pull me out with your damn tweezers,
and hope I disappear for good.
It was never the hot wax that burned me,
it was always your shame.
You trapped me inside of you—
shoving me all over the place, pretending so hard
to be the woman you already are.

Hello? Give me back the mic?
I'm here to make eye contact with you.
I make a clear request:
Please. stop. burning. me. with. your. rage.
And bring your kindness to me.

What was that? Yes —
you are a woman.
I am the letters "h" and "e" safely inside of your "she,"
asking for some space to speak.

Let's move forward,
I've got things to do, people to
become.

Please hand me the controls.
I promise I won't steal away your girlhood,
I won't take away your gigs,
those are yours to give up—

Just give me my joystick,
trust me.
I'll let your desire
always lead the way.
All I ever wanted
was to play.

Heroine's Journey Chapter 10

Integration of Masculine and Feminine

This final chapter is not one where we tie a bow at the end of this book. It is untying the notion that the inner masculine and feminine elements could ever complete their story at all. In this chapter, I cast myself to a new place that I call the Grand Ampersand, where both opposing forces are free to be themselves fully.

The more I let the masculine express desires to make something in the world, then the more the feminine has access to her deepest connectivity, sensuality, and presence – her desire to just be. This final chapter is about making space for these two opposing forces. A true internal marriage of a soul.

Masculine & Feminine

Today we celebrate the union
of woman and man,
the two living inside you.

Your virile hairy-chested man makes split decisions,
thinks once and then moves on.
Incisive, understanding his facts,
always axes down giant trees,
when their time has come.

The woman in you is supple, breathes inside your heart.
She is the soft dough that comes before bread.
She is the whisper of surrender.
She is the immense force of acceptance,
that opens your shut doors,
so she can pour her ocean of love
through you,
just for love's sake.

Light two candles,
let them become one single force,
merge them into an incandescence
that was you all along.

The Grand Ampersand

It is a car crash.
Blood is on the road, I have vanquished
hope.
Someone has been killed, and others are dying
still.

I am at a complete halt, unable
to forge ahead in fullness.
The devastation of a knee on a neck in Minneapolis,
a lack of oxygen in India, democracy in existential crisis,
let alone the trauma in my own story.

How can I take in
another sip of oxygen when the fumes of guilt
imprison me?

My freedom and joy are a true
embarrassment
of riches. I don't want to exhale either,
I may see my own shame,
that dark smelly haze from my breath
in the middle of summer.

I am stranded on the road,
unable to pass through
the dark moon of grief,
nor open my eyes to the sun.

What sun?

Inside of hopelessness, there is hope,
because **the truth lies**.
Here's the secret: there is a veiled passageway
up in the sky.
Its door is shaped
in the magical Grand Ampersand.

The portal of the ampersand is strong,
because it is where your wholeness lives.
You can feel both, together at the same time,

destroyed
&
joyful.

The more deeply you bow down to your heavy chest full of grief,
the more space laughter has to dance in your lungs.

The more you feel the warmth of happiness,
like honey smoothing its way down your throat,
then the more room you have to rage and rage.

The ampersand is not a seesaw,
one cannot reduce the other.

Its shape is a puzzle to find,
it's the infinity sign in total disguise.

You only have to breathe in on purpose to notice
The Grand Ampersand's veiled passageway.
As soon as you do, you're already
inside.

How to Bake your Future

Whenever I need,
I open the oven to bake my very future.
Mix up my first name with my dreams.
Season it with a taste of my thoughts,
never wasting an ounce of any ingredient.
Pour all of it into a well-loved round-ish pan.
This bakeware is dented from my rage,
scorched by old shame, cracked from sadness's weight.
It remains **wide open to all my substances**,
carrying them well.

I turn up the heat,
close my eyes
and wait.
I give myself time
to let all my parts seep
into my being.

I can never extract the Indian from inside.
I can never unscoop the American.

I wait for the truth to cook
into a single formation.

Me,
softened like the inside of a bubbling
pumpkin pie,

no longer difficult to digest,
with a crust firm enough
to contain me.

Delicious,
ready to be tasted,
ready to be seen,

ready to be shared.

Luxury Accommodations

Moving is always a pain:
boxes too heavy, dishes so many,
the opposite of sanity.

I step into the infinite horizon
to make it my forever home,
cozy in this un-still place, where I am also heading to.

I awake in my new location, and bear early morning
witness to a sane earth
casting herself towards her sun—
every morning is a sweet and slow-brewing homecoming.

Every evening, Happiness's sister, Sadness,
peers out from inside the sunset, surrendering my day
into its too-early, too-irreversible
end.

Every night, I accept sunset's final offer, a deep moonlit
tryst,
and her softly lit optimism, promising me tomorrow,
as I let myself **glide away**
from the same sun that soothes me.

My horizon is the line of infinite anticipation—
where new chapters are birthed,
a moving walkway
where conversations can pick up where they left off,

where the future I desire lives in my skin now,
where my next coming has already happened
in the pages of time,
and kismet is a tall green potted plant, living well in this all-windows residence.

This horizon is an enchanted kitchen where I drink tea made of hope,
where I am fueled by speaking only of possibility.

In these luxury accommodations, I can melt my view,
softening every part of my eyes
until the horizon is at home
in the real estate of my soul too,
where my scenery is always transforming,
where I am constantly changing,
excruciatingly new.

One Team

We were never alone.
My armor was never that thick.
In this immense universe, my neighbor lives
just on the other side of this
little rectangle wall.

It was always a duet, a trio, a quartet,
everyone with their own contributing vibration.

The audio waves of an entire population
make their way to me.

The roaring music recorded by the talent in London
moves my feet in Arlington.
I crave a chocolate croissant
made by an early morning baker in Paris.

A fresh pie crumbles on a plate in DC,
its ripe blueberries hand-picked
by a hard-working soul in New Jersey.

I sip fresh juice from a glass bottle
arranged on the shelf by a grocery worker.

We are all in the same dance.

There is only one team,
and **you were already picked**.

There is only one band,
making one magnificent human song.

Tune in to this cosmic ensemble.
Even the hopeful empty space around you
is the same space in a different galaxy.
It is the same empty space that sits within your own ribs.

There is no invitation,
you already belong.

The Opposite of a Pre-Nup

The man I want,
he wants all of me.
My ability to penetrate the world,
my vibrancy, my energy, my fears, my anger,
the whole fruit of me,
not just the sweet juice.
Tell me—
what's my half
of the deal?
It must be the opposite of a pre-nup.
What do I offer up,
so we can both roam wildly?

I promise to see you
if you need to pause,
milk life's poetry.
Listen to your trees, birds,
the heartbeat
of mother earth,
letting her rivers bring you to your knees.
I can be sturdy
in my femininity,
not just **make room**
for your softness,
the places where you are lost, your vulnerability.
I can invite it into my front door,
make a plate for it at my kitchen table,
lay its head down on the pillow of my heart.

I let you draw your sap
from your life's forest,
even develop a taste for it.

Shimmering With You

If your love is the sun,
I am the ocean, catching each ray,
reflecting it back into space.

Delighting in you,
shimmering with you
in your love.

I am not my Trauma, I am not my Healing either

My jaw is no longer locked
with the hurt I was working too hard to erase,
chewing and chewing on the raw material
of my feelings all day.

I am not my trauma.

When I was born, I was expelled
from a warm womb
into a cold room.
I screamed it all out.
I wish to learn from that day.

Push the river of pain out through my body
with a shake, a scream,
shivering it out
from my mouth, from my muscles.

I am not my healing either.

My brain, and my whole head was glued to solving
figuring it out, and solving some more,
turning the healing into tension,
instead of the other way around,
making it into a monster project.

I can, instead, **accept it all**
radically,
just like the wise ocean lets its beloved old whale

fall to the ocean floor,
releasing itself from carrying
the death it had witnessed.

This too shall pass, they always say.
But first, I must let it be.

Forgiveness

What is it that divides me from you,
but a spectacle of time?
It's a few breaths of air even,
between our many conversations.

I have enough compassion to warm us both up.

So, what is it that divides you from me,
but the dying embers remaining after a kind, warm fire?

The heat that might remain after a hug,
weighing nothing, carrying with it only
that moment before we were introduced into each other's
dances;
well before our muscles tightened
into tense choreographies.

What is it that divides me from you,
but that one moment before we met,
before life gave us our particular duet?

The Turtle Poem

A turtle does not hide.
and she also does not seek
her shell from fear, hesitation, or shame.
She simply found **a place to rest** inside of herself.
That's the secret behind her little smile.

Giraffe Poem

A giraffe is beautiful, not because she is tall,

but because she commits to staying lifted.

She chooses to **sip only elevated air**.

She relies on the strength of her

v
u
l
n
e
r
a
b
l
e

neck.

Even when she is still, she persists

in breathing from her highest,

her most inspired,

her only self.

How To: Self-Care Shower

In the evening when I wash my hair,
I rinse out
the day and every yesterday.

My long locks are my destiny
persisting as they wish,
miraculously
without my will.

I soothe this passageway
of time, taking good care
of my rooted hair.

I massage
soapy words
straight into my scalp—
I'm sorry.
Please forgive me.
I'm sorry.
Please forgive me.

I want to sleep knowing
that in the morning,
I will be in **decent standing**
with myself.

I ease my future
with the good conditioner:
Thank you.
I love you.
Thank you.
I love you.

Dear Earth, a Gratitude Poem

I sometimes wonder
how it is that I am not grateful
every waking moment.
Planet earth's center of gravity
keeps calling for me,
keeps accepting me,
even as I stamp my feet in anger upon her surface,
as I tiptoe to hide myself within her care,
tickling her body as I tremble in my fear,
and as I laugh loudly in her space.
I am carried so **lusciously**.
I am wanted so openly.
I am held

exactly as I am already.

Dear earth and your gravity,
thank you for having me.

song of dance

this world used to choreograph me.

i waited for the rain to fall to fake my sadness.
i waited for the sun to rise to force my lightness.
i waited for others to laugh to cue my smile.
i'm a dancer and i let this world choreograph me.

when all the drivers turned right, i hesitated to make the left.

now this body screams
for her freedom, so i stopped all the cells in my body from moving.
i paused to make a true move, waited in silence for my next impulse
until i could hear my pulse.

when i dance, i pour water into the river to give it my own rhythm.
when i dance, **everyone else stretches to a new height**.
when i dance, repenting white daffodils turn pink
from forgiveness.

when i dance, summer comes a day early.
when i dance, all the strawberries of the world get sweeter.
when i dance, a familiar spark inside grows into
a warm fire;

i do not kill time, i listen to time, make time,
move with
time, and see an entire world
choreographed by me.

You are Enough

There is a star out in space,
completely unaware how we are dazzled
by her light,

held together by her own gravity,
a presence to behold.
She is enough—
for simply existing.

Acknowledgements

I've learned that creating a life of discomfort is easy to do alone. However, doing something fulfilling like making a life-long dream come true absolutely required a team. I am indebted to those who have spent their hearts, minds, and souls in helping create my first book.

An exceedingly enthusiastic thank you and standing ovation for opening your heart and letting me walk inside and have a seat, to exchange inspiration, igniting me into this new phase as an author: *Allyson Hernandez, Ashley Hammond, Dana Maas, Jeffrey Kluger, Lauren Sabol, Morganne Davies, Nisha Kapadia, Nivi Achanta, Philip Attar, Reshma Naik, Scott Morgan, Steve Litzow.*

Thank you Susan Quatrone and Bela Shah Spooner for being constants in my open-mic audiences way back when.

Thank you to the life-giving team at Georgetown Creator's Institute and New Degree Press: *Samuel Hawkins II, Bailee Noella, Blake Hoena, Erika Nichols-Frazer, Jordan Waterwash, Aislyn Gilbert, Elissa Graeser, Gjorgji Pejkovski, Eric Koester,*

Hayley Newlin, Lyn S.,Tiffany Mosher, John Saunders, Stephen Howard, Brian Bies.

Thank you to draft editors: *Shenon Hahn, Richard Peabody.*

Thank you to my early excerpt readers: *Ariana Prawda, Esperanza Gene, Ify Bụjé, Melody Valdez, Pranjal Jain, Ruth Littlejohn, Shanthi Blanchard.*

Thank you for the boost of extra support to: *Alexandra Taliaferro, Anagha Dwivedi, Bethany Vance & Kyle Kosinski, Dana Saydak, Eric Pliner, Mark Mercer, Team FOT.*

I am in deep gratitude to my early donors, without whom this book would not be possible. Thank you for trusting me.

Akansha Agrawal, Alexandra Taliaferro, Alicia Kellstrom, Allison L Ross, Allyson Hernandez, Alyson Rixner, Amanda Caruso-Yahne, Amar Mehta, Ami Sonawala Naidu, Amy Malinski, Amy Warren, Ana Clara Salles Abreu de Paiva, Anagha Dwivedi, Andria McQueen, Anurag Mehta, April Moss, Apurvi and Manthan Shah, Ariana Prawda, Ashley Hammond, Ashika Kapoor, Ashley Hammond, Ayu Hartini, Bela Shah Spooner, Bengi Manley, Bharat Ranjan, Bobbie Motiwala, Brenna McDonough, Brian Feldman, Bethany Vance and Kyle Kosinski, Caren Quinn, Carly and Patrick Coleman, Carolee Doughty, Charles Hart, Chitra Panjabi, Christa Mannino, Coree Cornelius Cynthia Nair, Dana Maas, Dana Saydak, Deverie Samuels, Dilip Amin, Dipali MacAllister, Elizabeth Royal, Em Gat, Jignasa Gusani, Emily H. Landsman, Emma Davis, Eric Koester, Eric Pliner, Erin Olsen, Esther Letsche, F. Scott Piro, Falguni Patel, Freddie

Matara, Gaye Pauroso, Graciela Thomen, Graham Pilato, Jack Quirk, Jackie M Steven, James Whalen, Jane St. John, Jasmine Vicencio, Jazzy B, Jeannie Baumann, Jeffrey Kluger, Jennifer Knight and John Nilsson, Jessica Hazard, Jessica Jellies, Joan Cuenco, John Robinson, Joule Mosteller, Julianne Brienza, Julie Garner, Kal Patel, Kevin Gandhi, Kinnari Patel, Kinnary Pandya, Kirby Duncan, Kirti Pujari, Krystyna M. Reign, Lata Patel, Leena Pendharkar, Lynley Mackay, Manpreet Dhanjal, Mariam Reardon, Marion Sindoni, Mark Mercer, Mark Otto, Matthew Schwartz, Melanie Mitchell, Melissa Shukla, Melissa Subt, Melody Valdez, Michael Prichard, Michelle Weavil, Milie Gusani, Monica Thakrar, Monique Gaw, Natasha Acosta, Neal Shah, Neelu Milak, Neha Mathew, Neha Shah, Nidhi Jaisoor, Nihar Chhaya, Niraj Mehta, Nisha and Mitul Kapadia, Nivi Achanta, Noelle Reese, Parag Sheth, Pascale Michel, Pooja Chawla, Perry Lindstrom, Philip Attar, Priya Hunter, Rachana and Vipul Bhatt, Rachell Kitchen, Rahul Das, Raj Pandya, Rasha Goel, Reena Borwankar, Reshma Naik, Richard Peabody, Robin Sukhadia, Roshni Patel, Sagina Wahi, Sandy Nunes, Sapan Modi, Sarah Simon, Scott Morgan, Shally Mohite, Shashi Bellamkonda, Sheetal Chhaya, Shefali Jaiswal, Simit Patel, Seth Marbin, Sonia Ashok, Sonia Wilson, Stefanie Barrett, Stefanie Kowitt, Stephanie Maschek, Stephanie Rickey, Stephen Elmore, Steve Litzow, Sue Allen, Susan Ganeshan, Susan Quatrone, Sushila and Dahyalal Patel, Swati Boggi, Tegan Holtzman, Tejal Levitt, Teresa Savin, Tina Rao, Toni Cowan-Brown, Tony Vanchieri, Trupti C. Gandhi, Valerie Kamath, Vicky Bhandari, Vinita Mujumdar, Vinod Valloppillil, Wayne Beekman, William F. Lawler, William Kurz, Wright Seneres, and Yasmeen Ibrahim.

Other sources of inspiration I am ever grateful for:

- *Rage Becomes Her* by Soraya Chemaly
- *The War of Art* by Steven Pressfield
- David Mura
- Asian American Literature Festival
- *Cuz I Love You,* album by Lizzo
- *Good Girl Gone Bad,* album by Rihanna
- *Masala Podcast*

Finally, thank you to the talented cover designer Milan Krstevski, to the cover photographer Joshua Pelta-Heller of Koala Photography, and to the skilled eye of the layout designer Mateusz Cichosz.

CPSIA information can be obtained
at www.ICGtesting.com
Printed in the USA
JSHW011128060323
38513JS00001B/3

9 781637 308141